THE RISE OF
THE MODERN
WOMAN

PROBLEMS IN CIVILIZATION

THE RISE OF THE MODERN WOMAN

Edited with
an Introduction by

Peter N. Stearns

Carnegie-Mellon University

FORUM PRESS

Published simultaneously in Canada.

Printed in the United States of America.

Library of Congress Catalog Card Number: 78-56350

ISBN: 0-88273-404-0

CONTENTS

INTRODUCTION

Women have experienced a vital series of changes during the past two centuries, and their implications remain to be fully worked out. The first shock of change was encountered near the outset of the nineteenth century, primarily in Western Europe and North America. Industrialization and urbanization set a new stage for women. This was true for the male minority as well, but change was to have a differential impact on the two genders. Novelty was most obviously thrust upon women, who were pressed into new work situations and new residences, for which they were supposed to assume prime responsibility, and exposed to new educational systems and political movements. But women also served as direct agents of change, particularly in alterations of family structure and functions but also, especially after 1850, in the broader society, forging new efforts at legal and political reform and seeking new systems of health care. In diverse areas of endeavor, not always in unison, women were on the move.

From the vantage point of the late twentieth century, and not assuming that the modern woman is even yet fully formed, one can see in the nineteenth century a number of false starts in the female reaction to the varied trappings of industrialization. False starts, that is, in that a number of crucial nineteenth-century developments were to be seriously modified, indeed repudiated by the most articulate women, during the twentieth century. This is why the nineteenth century, flexibly construed, serves as a convenient first period in the passage of women from traditional to modern. By 1914 women had completed the pattern of initial adjustment, and some strained to move more quickly and in more novel directions. By the 1920s important elements of nineteenth-century women's culture, especially those subsumed under the heading "Victorian," had become the enemy, attacked as degrading to the x-chromosomed gender.

But the nineteenth century is not a museum piece in women's modern evolution, though there is a tendency still to look at some aspects of Victorianism as oddities from which the twentieth century in its wisdom has escaped. Most historians see the nineteenth century as integrally tied to woman's history right up to our own day. Features of "Victorianism," objectionable to some, persist, for nineteenth-century female culture took deep roots; Mother, in its modern connotations as a nineteenth-century product (crowned with her own "Day" by the U.S. Congress in 1917), is still with us, for example, however confining the maternal role may seem to some. Other nineteenth-century developments, such as the first widespread adoption of artificial contraception as a means of birth control, seem basic to the modern woman even freed from any specifically Victorian trappings. Finally, it can be argued that insofar as women in the nineteenth century seemed to cling to many established roles, even to glorify them, they adapted quite rationally to the massive changes in their environment, more rationally than men who, voluntarily or under compulsion, exposed themselves more obviously to the cutting edge of industrial society; more rationally, some contemporary women would hold, than those of their sisters who now challenge the substantial role differentiation between genders.

Any such basic and complex century of change must provoke extensive historical debate. A serious subject, vital in any understanding of the contemporary human animal, attracts powerful minds, and these carve out their own particular expressions. Though a rather new field of study, women's history already bears the mark of this process. And historians, again like other serious researchers, know that controversy is the stuff of professional life, at once advancing knowledge and venting professional egos. Controversy in women's history is fueled by two additional factors. The latter half of the twentieth century is witnessing a truly dramatic upheaval in women's roles and male/female relations, directed both *toward* greater fulfillment of lines sketched a hundred years before and *against* certain basic adjustments set out in the earlier century of change. Since 1940 ever increasing numbers of married women have sought and found formal employment, for example, against the preponderant nineteenth-century trend to withdraw wives and mothers from formal jobs in reaction to industrial change. Yet this is no mere revival of preindustrial patterns, where women, like men, worked in the family economy, for the current development is based on nineteenth-century creations such as artificial birth control and a new sense of women's individuality in law and in life. Interpretation of the nineteenth century is inevitably colored by present diversities and conflicts; nineteenth-century woman almost inevitably becomes a foil for what the observer thinks twentieth-century woman is or should be. The fearful may see the nineteenth century as a haven of respectability, when good women stayed home; the optimistic may see current trends as a logical fulfillment of nineteenth century patterns — modern woman moving confidently, ever forward; the strident may view the nineteenth century as a cruel hoax, with women enslaved, even newly enslaved, by men who saw in them only a secure anchor against the outside world — and as such, a century to be understood in order to be rebelled against, toward a new, proper social environment.

Second, modern women's history is itself new, and novelty always engenders fruitful debate as basic guidelines are sought. Women's history represents a real anomaly in conventional historiography: a topic so important to the understanding of both past and present that serious issues follow almost automatically as one comes to grips with a huge segment of the human experience, and yet a topic so new that an air of uncertainty remains, leaving room for more than repetitions and reassertions of conclusions developed previously. Notably, key camps are not established along strictly conventional lines such as Marxist and non-Marxist. A Marxist must argue that the situation of women in the nineteenth century was poor, given capitalist preponderance, but so may a non-

Marxist, influenced by a desire to see a major upheaval of roles within advanced capitalist societies. Both can (but need not) agree on the particular plight of working-class women, whether because of capitalist exploitation of the entire class or because of a particularly virulent male dominance. Classic ideological camps are not the key to most of the debates over women's history in the recent past.

The novelty of women's history is familiar, but it really should be surprising that the subject was not explored long ago. The careful historian, of course, rushes in to add that not all women's history is new, that important statements emerged, for example, during the first, late-nineteenth-century round of feminism or as an offshoot of the Marxist critique of the artificial subordination of women in society. Yet, granting some orientation from earlier evaluations and a few serious factual studies (mainly on factory women), almost all the controversies involved in women's history have developed within less than two decades. They have an immediacy but also a rawness that few other topics have, and probably none so significant, can claim.

The surge of interest has, obviously, followed from the new, second round of feminism. Feminists with different visions for the future see different pasts. A few comparative conservatives have seen the recent past in terms sufficiently positive to serve as an argument against the need for massive, induced change in the present. Ongoing trends, in other words, are basically good and already fundamental. Few *real* conservatives, however, have entered the lists, beyond some brief editorial dismissal, for women are simply not important enough in their eyes to require sober historical study justifying the status quo or the good old days; male oppression, if such there has been, has seen few explicit historical defenses, unlike nineteenth-century capitalism or slaveholding which have won serious, at least partially sympathetic treatment. The *relative* conservatives mostly say that things are changing already in the right direction and have been doing so since at least the nineteenth century. All this gives the modern history of women a distinctive cast, for we need not dally too long with arguments between and among Marxists, liberals, and conservatives. The debates and the very terms of debate are new, vibrant — and profoundly important.

For the history of women in its present dimensions is not the product of new-wave feminism alone. To be sure, its practitioners are disproportionately American (dealing with Europe as well as the United States), just as the most vigorous feminism is; Europeans have been slower to pick up the history of women as a special focus for examination and controversy. But women's history is a product of what some call the "new" social history as well. For about three decades, and with serious precedent earlier, social historians have striven to capture the entirety of the human experience in the past: not just politics or formal ideas but birth, death, love, play, and work. Though few had carried their inquiries into special consideration of women — definitely a comment on the male-centeredness of even innovative historians of both genders — the new consciousness of women's significance and strivings meshed well with this historical approach. And to this extent, in turn, women's history has served not just to enhance women's consciousness of themselves or a particular argument about women's future roles, both worthy enough, but to satisfy a quest for basic understanding of the human animal. Hence, as most women's historians note, women's history is vital for the history of any society, indeed for the history of men themselves.

A serious inquiry into the history of women's history would note efforts, some of them continuing, to deal with women's past in terms other than sociohistorical. Happily, we do not pretend a history of history, which can resemble a Hollywood portrayal of a fabled director — fascinating for the profession but "so what" to those outside it. Important histories of ideas about women (Marx, John Stuart Mill); of women's politics (reform movements, feminism); and "great" women of the past (George Sand, Florence Nightingale) exist and are still be-

ing produced. They relate but are not central to the serious stuff of women's social history, that is, the history of how most women acted in the past and, to the extent possible, how they viewed their lives.

In these areas lie the important current issues, as to what the nature of women's work, family life, and social goals were and, through these topics, what was the nature of the reaction to modernity. The history of great women or ideas about women has often been framed in terms of a need, now disappearing, to justify attention to women in the eyes of conventional, usually male, historians: women had a Queen Victoria to men's Abraham Lincoln; Mill thought about women's rights as well as liberty and equality, and Mary Wollstonecraft thought about them, too.

Social historians in any field would argue that the study of "great" people must always be integrated with an understanding of broad popular currents, that politics and complex ideas must be assessed as they resulted from or affected key social groups. This approach is all the more vital in women's history, although it does pass quickly over some solid work on women's political and intellectual history and biography, because conventional history until quite recently has been in fact so overtly male. Unless one is content to claim that behind every great man there is a woman or to distort beyond reason the signifiance of those women who had an impact in conventional male terms (the queens, the female novelists), one must look toward developments rooted in the seemingly ordinary lives of large groups of women. So, for the nineteenth century, historians turn increasingly toward substantial changes in family, in sex life, in work patterns, many of which flowed from women and all of which affected them. In a real sense we look at the common activities of women to undertand their basic approach to life in the past and indeed, as it proved durable, into the present day. Correspondingly, the leading historical issues involve the fundamental direction of women's social participation in modern times, how they spent most of their lives and directed most of their thinking, which in the nineteenth century proved highly creative.

Yet here we begin to get at some of the concrete terms of debate within social history itself. Were the new extent and methods of birth control due to formal ideas and propagandists, whether feminists urging female freedom from maternal drudgery or Malthusians bent on reducing population pressure? Or did they stem from a new dynamic of family life, so that ordinary women not only adopted change but in a basic sense caused it? A dramatically new situation resulted, we can all agree, but its relationship to a broad new conception of woman's family role relates crucially to the issue of causation and this in turn relates to an assessment of the depth and nature of the alteration of the lives and outlook of ordinary women in the mid-nineteenth century. We face similar interpretive problems today. Is a new evaluation of women's role the result of feminism, a trickle-down theory of causation, or from significant developments that began before the new wave of feminism, notably widespread work outside the home by married women? This is not an idle debate of which came first but is vital to an understanding of how deep and how far change has gone and is likely to go. If women were changing on their own, for example, they might integrate new work roles in an otherwise recognizable view of life; but if they depend on feminism for redefinition, their newly acquired ideas have revolutionary potential for Western society.

Here indeed is the first sweeping problem in assessing women's nineteenth-century history: did women's life evolve or was it revolutionized? There are implications for our own day in this question, for if fundamental change occurred a century ago, we may assume that we are probably just working out its consequences. But if only a mild adaptation to a new environment occurred, we may need, or be forced to face, a fundamental reevaluation of women's role right now. Historical debate is no idle exercise in this case, for figuring out what has happened is one key to figuring out what is happening now.

No historian has claimed that women were changeless in the nineteenth century, and most would cite great changes indeed. Early work on women pointed to the radical newness, often to the brutal newness, of the factory setting; surely female factory workers were involved in a total upheaval. More recently some historians have cited areas in which women long maintained contact with tradition, particularly by working in the home as housewives, servants, or even domestic manufacturers, each a category embracing far more nineteenth-century women than the factories employed. From this one could argue that women evolved, adapting traditions, rather than being forced to their abrupt abandonment. Or that fundamental change occurred only late in the nineteenth century, after tradition had cushioned the first shock. Or, more subtly still, that maintenance of traditions such as home-centeredness was in fact revolutionary in itself because the outside world changed so rapidly; women were being shut out of the things in life that were now important, compelled even in the twentieth century to struggle to recapture some of their customary place in society as a whole by casting aside traditions that barred access to the real rewards of modern society.

Evolution-revolution constitutes a common framework for historical debate, as some delight in finding novelty while others seek continuities; its familiarity, however, should not conceal its importance in nineteenth-century women's history. And the issue leads readily to the next debate: was change good or bad? Subjective judgment is frowned upon by many historians, who properly seek objectivity free from concern for good or bad, but on the subject of women's social history subjective considerations seem almost unavoidable. Evolution, for example, sounds good for those who see humans adapting to gradual change, but only if the starting point, in this case society before industrialization, was not too bad. If pre-industrial society was radically inadequate, revolution sounds better, though revolution can be jarring in itself, leading to significant if perhaps temporary problems of adjustment. But the question of whether nine-teenth-century trends were good or bad in-evitably relates to our own time, not to the past century alone, and this is where subjec-tivity enters with a vengeance.

If the historian finds promise in the cur-rent situation of women, he can either con-demn the nineteenth century — look how far we have come since — or praise trends whose present solidity owes much to nineteenth-century roots. If one chafes under contem-porary restrictions on women one ter.s to see nineteenth-century adjustments, such as glorification of the home, as cruel decep-tions made worse by their continuation to the present. (In strict logic it would be possi-ble to prefer the nineteenth century to the present — witness the absence of much fe-male protest until the century's end, in con-trast to current ferment — and seek ways in which nineteenth-century satisfactions have been eroded, but this theme has been devel-oped only by a few males who dismiss the whole subject with a feeling that women were happy then and if they had any sense should still be so today.) Subjectivity, was it good or was it bad, derived in large measure from perceptions of the present, must here impinge on the past. A shame, perhaps, for disinterested truth but also a statement that women's history has meaning for us, which is why we must judge it. Which is the same as saying that labeling an argument "fem-inist," i.e., partisan, is not the same as prov-ing that it is specious. Precisely because we must know women's past to know their fu-ture, tag words cannot be used to dismiss an approach; we are all partisan here to some degree.

Coming to terms with subjectivity in-volves a subsidiary issue: what are the pre-sumed standards of measurement? If women improved their lot in the nineteenth century, was this from an awful preindustrial base? This could mean that the nineteenth century was still pretty bad in absolute terms (estab-lished by some package of values rooted in a sense of what should be). If women's lot de-teriorated, was this because the eighteenth century had been exceptionally good? Or was women's lot always bad, at least in West-

ern society? This latter idea tends again to a judgment in absolute terms and suggests that the nineteenth century is really a slump in the middle of a deep trough.

There are several logical possibilities about the context of values and preindustrial history in which the nineteenth century must be placed and which form a basic peri-odization, or trend assessment, for the cen-tury itself. Given the fact that some features of women's life did begin to change rapidly, if not in the century as a whole at least by its end, one can picture a movement 1) stead-ily upward from preindustrial society: purga-tory giving way to redemption; 2) steady de-terioration: a golden age giving way to rot; 3) temporary perdition, from which women are now heroically emerging; or 4) a more subtle, delayed reaction, but ultimately in one of the directions suggested above. The mutations are numerous but constitute more than an exercise in ratiocination, for they follow from assessment of key facts in a new field: when and in what direction, for example, did family life really change for women? Further, to get at direction, some priority must be assigned to the various facets of women's lives, even under the rub-ric of social history. For example: should we look at servants (more numerous) or factory women (more novel) as the primary basis for assessing change in work? Should women's evolution-revolution by judged by family life, or is this copping out by selecting one of the most obviously female realms? Should one, instead, emphasize neutral or seemingly male-oriented criteria which are in fact more relevant in measuring women's true impor-tance and satisfaction, such as the quality and rewards of work, or legal status, or polit-ical strength? Plus, again, the vital question of judgment by what standards: are things good or bad now, and how does this relate to the past?

And from subjectivity comes credit or blame, implicit at least in most of the discus-sions in this book. If women's lot was bad (a judgment in absolute terms) or getting worse (compared to a specific historical standard, usually preindustrial society), who was at fault? Maybe women themselves were at fault, for making unfortunate if understandable choices. Maybe men, or some men, for using their authority to press their daughters or wives or subjects into confining roles. But if men were at fault, were women simply docile dupes? or were they explicitly repressed, powerless to combat the evil coming from without? Did they in fact protest, in which case late nineteenth-century feminism can be seen as an explosion prepared by decades of frustration and/or other, more neglected expressions of discontent can be sought earlier. (Of course life may be unhappy anyway for most people of both genders, which would make a bad nineteenth century unsurprising in the chronicle of human misery; but this level of pessimism, common in traditional Christian historiography, is unfashionable today, because when things must be improvable a bad or deteriorating period has to be explained, preferably in terms of removable human failings of the subjects themselves — women, or more commonly some oppressors; here men, some men, or male values and institutions.) But if things were getting better, were women creative enough to be the cause (extreme optimism), or did other factors play a role at least in setting the ball rolling? Again the new birth control measures provide an obvious case in point. We know they did develop, but did male publicists, inventors, doctors, or just plain husbands or lovers take the lead, aided perhaps by an exceptional woman or two? Or did birth control follow from the evolving or revolutionized needs and aspirations of large numbers of women? If the former, birth control might initially have been a shock, beneficial to women only in the twentieth century when values shifted from an exclusive maternal focus; hence, again, a view of the nineteenth century as an especially troubled period.

But if significant numbers of women sponsored birth control, in addition to being obviously affected by it, the direction of recent history looks different. Women run their own show, with the advent of industrialization, and fashion their own fate in what really matters, implicitly against men or at least independent of them, and if an even better

twentieth century followed as a result, optimism would seem logical, unless one espouses male supremacy or even simple mutuality. Both lines of argument, interestingly, can be feminist, just as in fact nineteenth-century feminists argued over whether birth control was a male plot or a vital boon. The first: the past was bad, male-dominated, even if it produced useful results which women now can and should build upon. The second: the recent past was already an improvement because women forged their own context, though of course this can and should be further elaborated, for in what is really important to women males were already becoming mere adjuncts. A debate on such a point is factual: when did new contraceptive devices develop, for what reasons, appealing to what motives? But it must involve a question of what women's life should be like and who should direct it, which hinges upon the sense of what women are doing and should do at present, what powers they have and should have over their own lives. This is all the more true in that subjectivity can so easily, and with the best intentions, be concealed. After all, the optimists might say, we are not facile feminists in claiming that women decided essentially on their own to limit births through artificial contraception. We are not claiming that men had oppressed, and we paint a happy picture of women in modern times. But the notion that "women should control their own bodies," which one can point to as a growing female achievement, is quite new, debatable on religious grounds or even in terms of equity in an area where men too, though unable to bear children, may have legitimate interests. All of which is to say that the debate is new, in some ways unrefined, and vitally tied to evolving disagreements over what women should be and therefore what they were in the past. Subjectivity again, and the resulting search for dupes, villains, or heroines (even collective heroines like womankind).

We focus, then, on classic historical issues applied to women's nineteenth-century history: change from what and toward what; evolution or revolution, in directions good, bad or (rarely) indifferent; and as a result of who or what causing what.

Four final problems must be raised before we trace the issues in specific historical statements: the question of sources, the question of geography, the relevant social stratification, and the construction of "models" of historical explanation.

Sources are always involved in historians' debates, for the subject is empirical in some measure, and usually in considerable measure. "Most women," like most men, are inarticulate to the historian in any direct sense; they did not leave explicit documents of record. But all sorts of people wrote about and for women in the nineteenth century. Reformers, particularly feminists, pointed to difficulties in women's situation. Some male doctors and other publicists attacked "modern" women and urged a variety of measures ranging from a return to religion and humility to radical medical practices designed to control female excesses. This kind of literature can be used to show how odd, repressed, or indeed maltreated nineteenth-century women were. But magazines, advertisements, and some pamphlets directed at women can be judged to show more creative responses to change. On an issue such as female sexuality, for example, the nineteenth century bequeathed a totally contradictory documentation, ranging from condemnations of sexuality or praise of women's supposed desire to abstain from non-procreative sex (and not to enjoy even procreative sex) to recommendations of sexual satisfaction. What sources correspond to what most women learned and believed and did? Statistics may help for some forms of behavior (illegitimacy rates or figures on age of marriage bear on sexuality); so may evidence on the types and numbers of readers of certain literature; furnishing, clothes, and artifacts are useful. But always the historian must choose, and here the choice determines positions concerning the direction of change but also may be in part determined by them. The historian who wants to find signs of oppression has little difficulty, any more than the historian who seeks to show successful adaptability. And new sources do emerge in this field, as in the range of sex-advice literature now being discussed, which keeps debate not only lively but productive.

Where should always be as important a question as when. Most work on Victorianism naturally focuses on Britain, but the United States has raised virtually identical issues, so that Victorianism is applied in the nineteenth century to the whole Anglo-Saxon world. Continental Europe, which produced less feminism, has been less blessed with historical attention to women, but France, Germany, certainly Scandinavia produced comparable historical issues about a prudish sexual culture or female work situations as shaped by industrialization. For this topic it is imperative *not* to let the Atlantic be a major conceptual barrier. North American, English and to an extent French or German nineteenth-century women's history can be discussed in similar terms, for these areas shared a Western culture toward women and a common experience of extensive nineteenth-century industrialization. Similarity does not, however, mean identity. France, more traditionalist and with a Catholic background, differs from Britain; the United States may show some particularly distinctive traits. We are talking about a women's world that in the nineteenth century shared a definable range of characteristics, different certainly from Eastern or Southern Europe or the non-Western world, though these areas might reproduce some Western traits as they industrialized later (which is one reason to study the Western pattern as a possible precedent for trends developing more widely now). But we must be attuned to possible comparative differences, even when left implicit by authors dealing with a single country within the Western framework.

Women are women, and some historians of this subject talk as if few substantial distinctions need be drawn among them. But certain historians focus mostly on middle-class women, the wives and daughters of business and professional people; others talk of middle-class jobs, notably white collar work such as teaching or secretarial service, though these might be held by women of lower-class origins. Others generalize more on the basis of the urban working class of manual laborers, while a few take in rural women as well. To be sure, even historians, careful to recognize that they deal with the middle or the working class primarily, differ widely in their interpretations. But social level, like geographical base, must be tested in assessing the power of overall statements about nineteenth-century women's history. Sometimes apparent contradictions derive mainly from different social focus. But even here one must finally ask whether a common element to the female experience existed, beyond the most basic biology, or, more narrowly, what groups (like what places) are particularly representative and/or significant. All the social differentiation possible does not remove serious debate, but some controversy is clarified by attention to stratification.

For historians are, in their combined efforts, trying to figure out how and why women were changing — not just one group of women or women in a single country. Interpretation does depend on what place is selected as important or typical. It does depend on what social class is held to lead the way, and in the selections that follow we see diverse efforts to use both the middle and the working class as the bellwethers. It does depend on what topic is stressed, whether family, or work, or law. But ultimately there is an effort to establish basic models of change; here the level of generalization is becoming quite high for a subject so new. There is rough agreement on important elements of the new environment: factories, cities, new types of literature for women. But in dealing with women themselves we are offered models of evolution and models of revolution; models of deterioration and models of improvement; models which see men as villains and models that ignore men almost entirely except to suggest that women, mainly by their own efforts, changed more successfully than men did (and so lived longer, were less frustrated). What all this has in common is the effort to suggest a general direction, a model of change. Even specific factual debates, such as that over

who adopted contraception first, and why, and when, have implications toward a sense of where women were heading. The effort to establish lines of motion, patterns of female action and reaction as industrial society began to take shape, proves fascinating; few social historians of women have as yet lingered too long over narrow topics without some suggestion as to how they relate to a larger process of change.

In the present period of immense change, historians are trying to convey their own desire to know what modern woman is, how she got where she is, where she seems headed, and, often, where she should head. Because we differ on the present, we seek an anchor in the past; present and past thus interact in historical interpretation as they do in shaping actual developments in the future. The broad lines of discussion are not exercises in professional nit-picking or argument for argument's sake. They stem from the vital character and the vitality of women and of women's recent history alike.

The following selections are grouped under several successive headings. First, an overview, of the sort that can be produced by historians in a general history of women but also by nonhistorians writing on women today. Here the central issues of revolution vs. evolution and the direction of nineteenth-century change are clearly formulated. Nineteenth-century work comes next, for it provoked the first serious research in women's social history and continues to fuel sophisticated analysis. Work in industrial society offers some clear standards of interpretation: what the conditons were, what values were used to judge, to accept, or to condemn, employment opportunities. But the measurements of work have long been male, and there is a specific problem of figuring out how appropriate these are for women. Family life comes next, the category embracing the largest number of nineteenth-century women, for far more women married and mothered than held formal jobs, agitated for change, or even read. Judgments about women's role in the family, the nature and function of that role, abound. Generalizations about Victorianism are rooted in assessment of women in the family, but recently some serious challenge to the conventional picture has developed. Working-class families were not like those of the middle class, though some proponents of a clear Victorianism contend that they became more so over time. And now there is debate about the values and practices even of the middle-class home, the bulwark of role definition for male and female alike in the Victorian age.

Discussion of the family relates to discussion of sex. Distinctive attitudes toward sex have long been central to the image of Victorianism, and now they are the subject of lively debate. Were sexual practices moving in the same direction for working-class and middle-class women? Was Victorian prudery even applicable to the middle class? If not, how could so many historians, and so many Victorians themselves, long have believed it so? In the history of women's sex all the major issues of historical interpretation are combined. We can find evidence of dramatic change or of continuity, of a sexual culture from which the twentieth century

had to free itself, or of a culture that truly created our own sexual world. And the topic clearly feeds our own conception of what we are, how frustrated or oppressed by relics of a strange past, or how confident that we, as a society and as individuals, express deep-seated and durable historical trends. After family and sex a taste of the debate over birth control follows logically, for the discussion now involves how much women wanted sex as well as how much and why they wanted children.

A final section explores trends just taking shape in the later nineteenth century and relates them to the central features of family and work history that went before: the emergence of formal feminism, which necessarily rouses debate; new forms of work; and suggestions of new definitions of gender roles. All these topics raise the key issue of any study of nineteenth-century women: how the situation of a century ago points to the situation now, how it informs us on why we are as we are and what we are likely to become in this vital area of women's roles and of male-female relationships.

CONFLICT OF OPINION

"The evolution of woman's conditions is to be explained by the concurrent action of these two factors: sharing in productive labor and being freed from slavery to reproduction."

————SIMONE DE BEAUVOIR

"As soon as the functions of women were no longer narrowly linked to physiological factors and ... demographic and economic imperatives, a search for moral justification started. The role of women developed a 'sacred' character and any modification in it triggered off an ideological debate, so that at present all discussion of their position has moral and ideological overtones."

———— EVELYNNE SULLEROT

"As tasks such as clothesmaking and food processing were gradually transferred to factories ... the central economic role of women also declined. As male and female spheres became more polarized in reality, notions of 'masculine' and 'feminine' responsibilities became more entrenched."

———— WILLIAM CHAFE

"All women were regarded in the first half of the nineteenth century solely as potential mothers. The worker with her own earnings was, accordingly, an affront against nature and the protective instincts of man."

———— WANDA NEFF

"Traditional families, then, operating on long-held values, sent their daughters to take advantage of increased opportunities generated by industrialization and urbanization."

———— JOAN SCOTT AND LOUISE TILLY

"Victorian husband-wife relationships represented a triumph of role stereotypes over reality. Women were gaining increasing competence in the social and educational spheres: yet they were asked to play a role which demanded complete subordination of their selves to the ego of their husbands."

———— BERNARD MURSTEIN

"Women, through their reign in the home, were to sustain the 'essential elements of moral government' to allow men to negotiate safely amid the cunning, treachery and competition of the marketplace."

———— NANCY COTT

"As she escaped the burden of producing for the family, she assumed the responsibility of consuming for the family — a modern way of living. A wise observer of Victorian society noted that in the second half of the century it was the task of the English woman to expend the collective earnings of the whole English nation."

———— PATRICIA BRANCA

"Ideally women would produce children by parthenogenesis; failing that, male impregnation should take place in a dark bedroom into which the husband would creep to create his offspring in silence while the wife endured the connection in a sort of coma, thereby precluding any stigma of depravity which would have been incurred by showing signs of life. . . . Sex could be dematerialized by ignoring it."

—— DUNCAN CROW

"The central fact in the history of courtship over the last two centuries has been the enormous increase in sexual activity before marriage. . . . After 1800 the percentage of young women who slept with their boyfriends or fiancés rose steadily."

—— EDWARD SHORTER

"It seems evident that among these women sexual relations were neither rejected nor engaged in with distaste or reluctance. In fact for them sexual expression was a part of healthy living and frequently a joy."

—— CARL DEGLER

"When we look at the flight from parenthood from this point of view it is clear that it was very far from being a revolt of women. . . . It is not unreasonable to argue that the initiative for birth-control came from the men."

—— J. A. AND OLIVE BANKS

"The insistence on women's right to refuse often took the form of attacks on men for their lusts and their violence in attempting to satisfy them."

—— LINDA GORDON

"Inspired, perhaps, by the claims of the women's movement, often hard pressed by material need, and swept onward if not exactly upward by the swelling tide of industrialization, middle-class working women in the later nineteenth and early twentieth centuries drastically altered both their position and their outlook."

—— LEE HOLCOMBE

"Of course the position of women in 1840 was no worse, and in some respects better, than in 1790, but by this time they were becoming conscious of their disabilities and interested in removing them." –

—— WILLIAM O'NEILL

"The girls often were rebelling not in gladness but in anguish, almost despite themselves. Tormented by doubt and shame, they would have welcomed some more conventional role if only there had been one that could have satisfactorily contained their needs. But the conventions of femininity did not fit them."

—— PETER FILENE

I. OVERVIEWS

Simone de Beauvoir

THE SECOND SEX

The publication of this book, in 1952, was a major precursor of contemporary feminism, rousing great interest in the problems of women and directly stimulating Betty Friedan's *Feminine Mystique*, which helped launch the American movement for new rights for women. Simone de Beauvoir is a major figure in twentieth-century French literature and philosophy, a conscious of the link between history and the present. This selection on the nineteenth century stresses stark ambiguities in recent women's history, with liberating developments juxtaposed to continued enslavement and even new inequalities and exploitation. The question of the extent and basic direction of change is clearly posed; is it resolved? What still retards women's freedom?, and by what standards, historical or other, is freedom to be measured?

I T might well have been expected that the French Revolution would change the lot of woman. It did nothing of the sort. That middle-class Revolution was respectful of middle-class institutions and values and it was accomplished almost exclusively by men. It is important to emphasize the fact that throughout the Old Regime it was the women of the working classes who as a sex enjoyed most independence. Woman had the right to manage a business and she had all the legal powers necessary for the independent pursuit of her calling. She shared in production as seamstress, laundress, burnisher, shopkeeper, and so on; she worked either at home or in small places of business; her material independence permitted her a great freedom of behavior: a woman of the people could go out, frequent taverns, and dispose of her body as she saw fit almost like a man; she was her husband's associate and equal. It was on the economic, not on the sexual plane that she suffered oppression. In the country the peasant woman took a consider-

able part in farm labor; she was treated as a servant; frequently she did not eat at the table with her husband and sons, she slaved harder than they did, and the burdens of maternity added to her fatigue. But as in ancient agricultural societies, being necessary to man she was respected by him; their goods, their interests, their cares were all in common; she exercised great authority in the home. These are all the women who, out of the midst of their hard life, might have been able to assert themselves and demand their rights; but a tradition of timidity and of submissiveness weighed on them.

[In the Industrial Revolution] Woman regained an economic importance that had been lost since prehistoric times, because she escaped from the hearth and assumed in the factory a new part in production. It was the machine that made possible this upheaval, for the difference in physical strength between male and female workers was to a large extent annulled. As the swift growth of industry demanded a larger working force than the males alone could furnish, the collaboration of women became necessary. That was the grand revolution of the nineteenth century, which transformed the lot of woman and opened for her a new era. Marx and Engels gauged its whole range, and they promised women a liberation implied in that of the proletariat. In fact, "woman and the worker have this in common: that they are both oppressed," said Bebel. And both would escape together from oppression, thanks to the importance their work would take on through technological evolution. Engels showed that the lot of woman has been closely tied to the history of private property; a calamity put the patriarchate in place of the matrilineal regime and enslaved woman to the patrimony. But the industrial revolution was the counterpart of that loss of rights and would lead to feminine emancipation. . . .

At the beginning of the nineteenth century woman was more shamefully exploited than were male workers. Labor at home constituted what the English called the "sweating system"; in spite of constant toil, the workingwoman did not earn enough to satisfy her needs. Jules Simon in L'Ouvrière and even the conservative Leroy-Beaulieu in Le Travail des femmes au XIXᵉ, published in 1873, denounced odious abuses; the latter says that more than two hundred thousand women workers in France earned less than fifty centimes a day. It is understandable that they made haste to get out into the factories; besides, it was not long before nothing was left to do outside the workshops except needlework, laundering, and housework—all slave's work, earning famine wages. Even lacemaking, millinery, and the like were monopolized by the factories. By way of compensation, there were large opportunities for employment in the cotton, wool, and silk industries; women were used especially in spinning- and weaving-mills. The employers often preferred them to men. "They do better work for less pay." This cynical formula lights up the drama of feminine labor. For it is through labor that woman has conquered her dignity as a human being; but it was a remarkably hard-won and

protracted conquest. . . .

The situation of the workingwoman was so deplorable that Sismondi and Blanqui demanded that women be denied access to the workrooms. The reason for their condition was in part because women at first did not know how to defend themselves and organize themselves in unions. Women's "associations" dated from 1848, and at the beginning these were associations of industrial workers. The movement advanced very slowly, as these figures show:

In 1905, there were 69,405 women out of 781,392 unionized workers; in 1908, 88,906 out of 957,120; in 1912, 92,336 out of 1,064,413.

In 1920, there were 239,016 workingwomen and female employees unionized out of 1,580,967 workers; and among women farm laborers only 36,193 unionized out of a total of 1,083,957. In all, there were 292,000 women unionized out of a total of 3,076,585 union workers. It was a tradition of resignation and submission, a lack of solidarity and collective consciousness, that left them thus disarmed before the new opportunities that were opening up for them.

. . . In spite of prejudices, opposition, and the survival of an outdated morality, we have witnessed the passage from free fecundity to a fecundity controlled by the State or by individuals. Progress in obstetrical science has considerably reduced the dangers of confinement; and the pain of childbirth is on the way out. At this time—March 1949—legislation has been passed in England requiring the use of certain anesthetic methods; they are already in general application in the United States and are beginning to spread in France. Artificial insemination completes the evolutionary advance that will enable humanity to master the reproductive function. These changes are of tremendous importance for woman in particular; she can reduce the number of her pregnancies and make them a rationally integral part of her life, instead of being their slave. During the nineteenth century woman in her turn emancipated herself from nature; she gained mastery of her own body. Now protected in large part from the slavery of reproduction, she is in a position to assume the economic role that is offered her and will assure her of complete independence.

The evolution of woman's condition is to be explained by the concurrent action of these two factors: sharing in productive labor and being freed from slavery to reproduction. As Engels had foreseen, woman's social and political status was necessarily to be transformed. The feminist movement, sketched out in France by Condorcet, in England by Mary Wollstonecraft in her *Vindication of the Rights of Woman,* and taken up again at the beginning of the nineteenth century by the Saint-Simonists, had been unable to accomplish definite results, as it lacked concrete bases. But now, with woman in industry and out of the home, her demands began to take on full weight. They were to make themselves heard to the very center of the bourgeoisie. . . .

The fact that governs woman's actual condition is the obstinate survival of extremely antique traditions into the new civilization that is just appearing in vague outline. That is what is misunderstood by hasty observers who regard woman as not up to the possibilities now offered to her or again who see in these possibilities only dangerous temptations. The truth is that her situation is out of equilibrium, and for that reason it is very difficult for her to adapt herself to it. We open the factories, the offices, the faculties to woman, but we continue to hold that marriage is for her a most honorable career, freeing her from the need of any other participation in the collective life. As in primitive civilizations, the act of love is on her part a service for which she has the right to be more or less directly paid. Except in the Soviet Union, modern woman is everywhere permitted to regard her body as capital for exploitation. Prostitution is tolerated, gallantry encouraged. And the married woman is empowered to see to it that her husband supports her; in addition she is clothed in a social dignity far superior to that of the spinster. The mores are far from conceding to the latter sexual possibilities equivalent to those of the bachelor male; in particular maternity is practically forbidden her, the unmarried mother remaining an object of scandal. How, indeed, could the myth of Cinderella not keep all its validity? Everything still encourages the young girl to expect fortune and happiness from some Prince Charming rather than to attempt by herself their difficult and uncertain conquest. In particular she can hope to rise, thanks to him, into a caste superior to her own, a miracle that could not be bought by the labor of her lifetime. But such a hope is a thing of evil because it divides her strength and her interests; this division is perhaps woman's greatest handicap. Parents still raise their daughter with a view to marriage rather than to furthering her personal development; she sees so many advantages in it that she herself wishes for it; the result is that she is often less specially trained, less solidly grounded than her brothers, she is less deeply involved in her profession. In this way she dooms herself to remain in its lower levels, to be inferior; and the vicious circle is formed: this professional inferiority reinforces her desire to find a husband.

Every benefit always has as its bad side some burden; but if the burden is too heavy, the benefit seems no longer to be anything more than a servitude. For the majority of laborers, labor is today a thankless drudgery, but in the case of woman this is not compensated for by a definite conquest of her social dignity, her freedom of behavior, or her economic independence; it is natural enough for many women workers and employees to see in the right to work only an obligation from which marriage will deliver them. Because of the fact that she has taken on awareness of self, however, and because she can also free herself from marriage through a job, woman no longer accepts domestic subjection with docility. What she would hope is that the reconciliation of family life with a job should not require of her an exhausting, difficult performance. Even then, as long as the temptations of convenience exist — in the economic inequality that favors certain individuals and the recognized right of woman to sell herself to one of these privileged men — she will need to make a greater moral effort than would a man in choosing the road of independence. It has not been sufficiently realized that the temptation is also an obstacle, and even one of the most dangerous. Here it is accompanied by a hoax, since in fact there will be only one winner out of thousands in the lottery of marriage. The present epoch invites, even compels women to work; but it flashes before their eyes paradises of idleness and delight: it exalts the winners far above those who remain tied down to earth.

The privileged place held by men in economic life, their social usefulness, the prestige of marriage, the value of masculine backing, all this makes women wish ardently to please men. Women are still, for the most part, in a state of subjection. It follows that woman sees herself and makes her choices not in accordance with her true nature in itself, but as man defines her.

Evelyne Sullerot

WOMAN, SOCIETY AND CHANGE

A French sociologist here offers a sweeping view of modernization: traditional society has certain basic prescriptions regarding women's role, modern societies change the very foundation of these, and the only problem seems to be a lag accompanying the initial transition. Women's "nature" no longer dictates distinctiveness. And yet history shows its hand in continuing hesitations against a recognition of the inevitable; we have repeated suggestions of resolution, yet we seem still to be waiting for it! Can modernization defeat what one might call historical biology, as Sullerot expects? Sullerot provides a significant orientation toward evaluating the specific issues of nineteenth-century women's history, particularly on the interaction between culture and economics/physiology. If the problems of transition are still with us after 200 years, perhaps the outcome is less certain than Sullerot suggests and a complex history even more important than she implies.

At birth, every woman is endowed with sexual characteristics finding expression in her erotic and reproductive roles which are quite different from those of man. Moreover, she must adopt social attitudes that clearly define her as a woman: certain roles and certain social characteristics, of which most have no apparent relationship with woman's special physiology. Thus, in no country or society do women dress like men. Often the very language is different, for example, the female Californian Indians used to speak a special dialect in which almost every word was different from that used by the men. Many languages — Japanese is one example — still contain significant differences between male and female word endings. To a lesser extent the same is true for languages of Greco-Latin or Semitic origin in which adjectives and past participles have different endings when they refer to men or women.

Usually from childhood upwards women are given special tasks and duties. All these characteristics add up to a kind of *social sex* which defines woman's place in society just as much as does her biological sex. Following Margaret Mead, it is interesting to note that these characteristics, roles and attitudes which make up the social sex are not uniform in every culture. While, in the same animal species, all the males and all the females behave in the same way and take on the same roles in mating, in nest building, in rearing the young, in displaying the appropriate plumage or coat, the social symbols of femininity and female roles vary significantly from one human society to another. In one society, women do not work in the fields; in another, they are responsible for all agricultural labour. In one, the father dictates the education of his children; in the other, the wife has a near-monopoly over bringing them up. In one, trousers are an exclusively masculine garb; in another, feminine. Any inversion of those roles or characteristics creates a sense of scandal and an impression that the world is upside down. Indeed, it was under the general title 'The world upside down' that popular prints depicting social customs but reversing sexual roles were published in Flanders in the seventeenth and eighteenth centuries. Yet ethnology makes it clear that these conventions are relative to each society and that what is 'the right way round' for some, is 'upside down' for others. It was early noted by Strabo of the Germanic tribes that they divided tasks between men and women in a way which was 'quite the reverse of ours'.

Nevertheless, no society has so far avoided these distinctions, even though the interchangeability of male and female roles is ample proof of how artificial such distinctions are.

Yet these distinctions, rigid in primitive and traditional societies, are more fluid in modern, rapidly changing ones. In the latter, they are being increasingly challenged, generally by women themselves, who feel that such discrimination is not to their advantage. However, the division between the sexes is everywhere maintained. It is almost as if humanity wanted for ever to put off the time when the sexes would not be socially differentiated — a situation often wrongly confused with the sexless society.

Moreover, social change brought about by technical development, industrialisation, urbanisation and political upheavals always seems more rapid for men than for women. Thus, in traditional societies, the position of women is still fairly well delineated by the continued role division between the sexes. But, in modern societies, it is the time-lag between social change for men and for women which is the main index of role differentiation and consequently of the position of women in relation to men. For example, it is not very significant to note that in the United States almost all women have a driving licence and drive cars just like men, while elsewhere cars are driven mainly by men. It is only when motoring is universal and the ability to drive is commonplace, without prestige and relatively boring, that all women get a chance to do it. When cars were scarce and represented prestige and power, women were seldom allowed to own and use them. The same time-lag is found in access to the professions as they were founded one after the other during the process of industrialisation. It is found also in the exercise of civil rights and in the level of educational attainment. A study of statistics on illiteracy shows that in the vast majority of countries it is mainly to be found among women. However, in countries which are completely literate, it is at the level of secondary, technical and above all higher education that the time-lag is most evident between the mass of men and of women. It is not typically masculine to be able to read and typically feminine not to; it is not typically masculine to have a doctorate and typically feminine not to. What is more important than the performance of women in one country or another is either that this time-lag continues to exist between progress for men and for women, or that the gap is being closed.

Our societies are evolving further and further away from cultural patterns where tasks were distributed in a way which had some physiological justification, for example, in terms of the relative physical strength of men and women. Automation and other technical advances have increasingly done away with these logical justifications which used to be considered natural laws. The basis on which tasks, roles and rights are allotted to each sex and the justification of differences between them needs to be re-examined in modern society. The ways in which such differences are maintained, the degree to which they are accepted and the grounds on which they are challenged or attacked call for investigation.

It is clear that women are dissatisfied almost throughout the world and that a constant debate about their position is in progress. Almost every constitution proclaims equality of rights and responsibilities for citizens of both sexes. In practice the resistance to legal equality is remarkably strong, particularly as it comes from women as often as from men. The underlying reason is that the position of women has always or nearly always been defined in terms of their *role*. Women have always been given a specific role, mainly in the family, and their social role has evolved from it. . . .

As soon as the functions of women were no longer narrowly linked to physiological factors and ceased to be shaped exclusively by demographic and economic imperatives, a search for moral justification started. The role of women developed a 'sacred' character and any modification in it triggered off an ideological debate, so that at present all discussion of their position has moral and ideological overtones.

To a certain extent the present condition of women could be compared with that of developing countries in relation to the developed ones. The efforts to reduce the gap between rich and poor countries could be taken as a guide in creating equality between men and women. Nevertheless, such an analogy would fail to take account of the interconnexions and between moral prejudice and preconceived ideas and the economic

and legal issues which are inseparable from the 'the problem of women'.

An understanding of the present situation would not be complete without a knowledge, albeit slight, of the past. Certainly the emphasis should be on recent causes bringing about modifications in the position of modern women, and principally on demographic and economic causes. Even so we are still the heirs of antiquated notions which influence our thinking, and it would be wise to bear them in mind. . . .

Everywhere one hears of change in the situation of modern women, of the 'undermining of traditional values', usually with fears about the emergence of a new breed of women. There is no need to go further than the national press or women's magazines to become aware of this. At the same time it should be remembered that there is nothing new about these statements, as a glance at such magazines published over the last two hundred years shows. They are full either of laments or praise of women's development and the corresponding revolution in traditional customs. Every three months the same points of view are aired anew in our modern press: the position of women is changing so rapidly that the future of the world is endangered and moral standards may be threatened. All statements about progress in woman's lot are fraught with concern about the potential disruption of society. Even while such articles hypocritically applaud the advances made by women, and over-emphasise it at will, it is easy to perceive that they seek to instill fear of change, to magnify the eternal nature of feminine duties and to see it as the cornerstone of social stability. This choir singing in unison about the dire consequences of emancipation should be mistrusted. A content analysis of countless articles on woman's position over more than two and a half centuries yields curious results. It appears that throughout this period all changes were always resented as disastrous for morality. Grandmothers and great-grandmothers were virtuous, modern women are no longer so. (This was written in 1750 and in 1850 in almost exactly the same terms as it is today.) The belief lurks among men that the female golden age is firmly located in the past and that only prehistoric wives were perfectly moral and perfectly dutiful in accepting their "natural" station in life.

This great fear of women's emancipation has led to so many false interpretations of alleged change that extreme care is now essential. Only the study of the past can provide an exact assessment of this evolution. It can show whether women's status improved as a result of their own efforts or whether it merely reflected changes in society brought about by men, whether women have always followed or have been innovators. If they have only been followers throughout history, it is hardly worthwhile to outline their present position in contemporary society. But it does seem that a radical change has occurred in the modern world and that we are now standing on the brink of a profound transformation. How it will take place, which particular adjustment will trigger off a chain reaction throughout the whole structure, how it will affect society at large and the opposite sex — these are questions which can only be answered through the study of history and the replacement of myth by knowledge.

William H. Chafe

WOMEN AND EQUALITY

Here again the theme of evolution seems strong in this recent approach to American women's history, by a professional historian interested primarily in twentieth-century feminism. In culture, indeed, one can wonder if even a significant evolution has occurred, which returns to the question of how one is to evaluate the relationship between attitudes about women and other aspects of women's lives in the nineteenth century. Can culture be discussed as not capturing reality? As with de Beauvoir, statements on change in traditional work roles further complicate assessment of the direction of nineteenth-century developments, whether insofar as change did occur it was for good or for ill. Was preindustrial society basically sound, so that women stood mainly to lose from its passing?

One of the remarkable themes of women's history has been the constancy of prescriptive attitudes toward woman's "place" over three and a half centuries. Especially for white middle- and upper-class women it has been customary to define happiness as fulfilling the "biological destiny" of being good wives and mothers. The histo-

Reprinted from William H. Chafe, *Women and Equality*, pp. 15-16; 17-18; 20-22. Copyright © 1977 by Oxford University Press, New York.

rian Julia Cherry Spruill observed that in the South in the 17th and 18th centuries "unmarried persons were regarded as pitiable encumbrances" and that "the home was the only field in which superior women might distinguish themselves." The family, in turn, was generally perceived as a hierarchy, with the man as father and head, and women and children as his inferiors. Although Puritan New Englanders believed that such an arrangement mirrored a divine pattern, with man's role in the home similar to God's role in the universe, one did not have to be a Puritan to subscribe to the idea of patriarchy. "In truth," the 19th-century Southern sociologist George Fitzhugh observed, "woman, like children, has but one right and that is the right to protection. The right to protection involves the obligation to obey." If there was a model of perfection in such a world-view, it was the matron quoted in *The Spectator*, a periodical read widely in the colonies. "I am married," she wrote, "and I have no other concern but to please the man I love; he is the end of every care I have; if I dress, it is for him; if I read a poem, or a play, it is to qualify myself for a conversation agreeable to his taste. . . ."

With some shifts of nuance and emphasis, the same normative values also characterized 19th- and 20th-century attitudes toward women. *The Ladies Calling*, regarded as the most authoritative advice manual dealing with female behavior in the late 17th and the 18th century, instructed women to be modest, meek, obedient, and pious — qualities nearly identical with the piety, purity, submissiveness, and domesticity which the historian Barbara Welter has identified as principal components of the "cult of domesticity" in mid-19th-century America. By the 1920's, Patricia Graham has noted, these virtues had been updated to include "youth," pleasing "appearance," and "acquiescence" as well as domesticity, but the desired end product was substantially the same. When Adlai Stevenson told the graduating women of Smith in 1955 that their task was to "influence man and boy" through the "humble role of housewife," he was essentially repeating *The Spectator's* 18th-century injunction

that women should "distinguish themselves as tender mothers and faithful wifes rather than furious partisans." Since women's ideal role was to be supportive of their husbands, care for their children, and provide a haven from the troubles of the outside world, the idea that they might wish an independent life or career of their own seemed unnatural. . . .

In the overwhelmingly agrarian society of colonial America, there was little opportunity for a leisure class existence or a polarization of labor between the sexes. Women from all classes were centrally involved in the mainstream economic activities of the community. Crops had to be planted and harvested, animals tended, clothes made, gardens cared for, and food prepared. Even in households with many servants, the mistress spent her day coordinating work activities, keeping accounts, and planning how best to produce the goods required to satisfy the clothing and food needs of various members of the household. In most cases, of course, it was the women of the family who spun the yarn, wove the cloth, kept the poultry, made the butter and cheese, harvested the vegetables, and prepared the food. . . .

The harsh facts of demography made even less likely the actualization of the leisure-class ideal described in the normative literature. Many women bore ten or twelve children, frequently living to see half of them die. As Anne Firor Scott has observed, "From the standpoint of ordinary people, the essential theme of the eighteenth century experience was not so much achievement as the fragility . . . of life. Death was an omnipresent reality." Jane Franklin Mecom, sister of the more famous Benjamin, had lost four of her twelve children by the time she reached fifty-one. In the next year a daughter died, leaving in her care four grandchildren, two of whom also died in six months' time. Only two of Thomas Jefferson's six children lived to maturity. So frequent were infant and maternal mortality that many women lived in constant fear of pregnancy. Indeed, in light of the burden of childbirth and childcare and the major contribution made by women to the economic production of the household, it is clear that no more than a few women could aspire to the leisure-class ideal described in *The Spectator.*

Partly because of the prevalence of early death, women also played a significant part in the public economic life of the society. It was not unusual for a widow to find herself in charge of a large farm, merchant business, or a shop. Although the socialization of affluent women emphasized passivity and genteel manners rather than assertiveness and business acumen, the average woman met such challenges with little difficulty. Women ran groceries, practiced medicine, and served as midwives, teachers, nurses, and printers. In 1690 some 40 per cent of all the taverns in Boston were run by women, and, in the same year, city authorities granted more than thirty women the right to saw lumber and manufacture potash. Whether as the result of the untimely death of a husband, or through their own initiative, individual women functioned effectively in the world of commerce.

Still others contributed in notable ways to the world of public affairs. Margaret Brent, a noblewoman who came to Maryland in the mid-17th century, was a famous stateswoman of her day. Already well regarded for her management of huge family landholdings, she was appointed after the death of Governor Leonard Calvert as executrix of his estate. In that position she played a crucial role in resolving numerous political disputes — in the words of Julia Cherry Spruill, "Rescu[ing] the struggling little colony from certain disaster." Mary Musgrove performed similar diplomatic feats for the colony of Georgia. The daughter of an Indian mother and an English father, she mediated between the Creek Indians and the colonial government of James Oglethorpe, acting to maintain the peace and at critical moments, to rally Indian support to Oglethorpe's side.

Overall, then, a strangely distant relationship appears to have existed between received cultural norms about woman's "place" and the actual content of most women's lives. That the norms were not forgotten can be seen clearly in a note from Thomas Jefferson to his daughter. "Your last two letters," he wrote, "are those which have given me the greatest pleasure of any I have ever received from you. The one announced that you have become a notable housewife; the other, a mother." Furthermore, it was not unheard of for traditional norms to be invoked in a restrictive manner. Anne Hutchinson was expelled from Massachusetts not only for her religious views but for "acting the part" rather of "a husband than a wife" and for behaving in a way "not fitting" for her sex.

Yet for the most part, prescriptive attitudes appeared only indirectly relevant to women's daily lives, existing more as conventions to which homage was paid on ritual occasions than as injunctions women were expected to obey in their everyday activities. Attacks on prevailing norms were rare; but, then again, such attacks might not be pertinent if the norms were not perceived as an immediate impediment to the routines necessary to keep life going. Reality existed on one side, prescriptive norms on the other, and, as long as homage was offered where appropriate, the rest of life could go on as usual. The result was a variety of behavior among women which, although not contradictory to existing norms, nevertheless differed considerably from what one might expect from reading the prescriptive literature. . . .

Significantly, the major shift in the relation of norms to behavior accompanied the fundamental transformation of the nation's economy which occurred with the industrial revolution. From the point of view of male and female roles, the primary impact of industrialism was to separate the homeplace from the workplace. As tasks such as clothesmaking and food processing were gradually transferred to factories, and as craftsmen moved from their shops to larger manufacturing facilities, the household unit as the center of economic activity declined. With it, the central economic role of women also declined. Women continued to perform indispensable work in and outside of the home, but no longer was there the inextricable relationship of male and female labor as part of a common enterprise. As male and female spheres became more polarized in reality, notions of "masculine" and "feminine" responsibilities became more entrenched.

At the same time, the types of activities women engaged in divided more sharply along class and ethnic lines. For upwardly mobile middle-class families, especially, a wife who enacted the culturally prescribed role of full-time homemaker constituted a visible badge of having achieved middle-class status. The price of insisting on such an existence, however, was that wives and daughters of the middle class became removed almost totally from the workaday reality of women from other classes. Rebecca Harding Davis, a 19th-century novelist, vividly described the distance which resulted. In *Life in the Iron Mills* she portrayed the isolation of an upper-class millowner's daughter who each day gazed down from her window at the exhausted faces of workers streaming to and from the mills. Though incomparably advantaged in every way, the rich daughter nevertheless suffered bitterly her own "hunger to know" about the real life of those around her.

II. WOMEN AND WORK

Wanda Neff

VICTORIAN WORKING WOMEN

From the standpoint of overview, women's work seemed an area where dramatic change could be noted clearly in the nineteenth century, as compared to culture, though it can be debated whether the change was good or bad (and whether short term deterioration might be compatible with long term, fundamental liberation). Specific studies of work formed the first explicit branch of what we now see as women's history, and the following selection, written in 1929 by a British historian, is fairly typical. Neff sees nineteenth-century work forms as new, horrible if fascinating, yet possessed of some promise compared to purely traditional roles. The focus on factory workers is typical of labor history generally, and the sense of horror shares a typical radical dismay at conditions of work for all manual laborers. But are factory workers as important as Neff's attention suggests? And how do their conditions in fact compare with traditional standards of specifically women's work? Neff suggests the complexity of this problem in discussing why women moved to the factories in the first place. Judgment of the conditions they found in their new work is complicated by comparison not to their own past but to men's standards, accompanied by some shock that women had to work so hard at all; these criteria must be sorted out in any final evaluation. Were women different from men as workers, and were differences voluntary or compelled? Should women workers be judged by nineteenth-century cultural norms, or if not, by what standards? (The issue of morals, particularly, comes smack against the problem of whether to judge by "official" nineteenth-century culture or by our own looser values; whether early factory work was good or bad hinges in part on this one choice.) Perhaps most important, how can we know what women themselves thought about their work, for on this vital point Neff suggests several possible judgments that lead toward radically different assessments of where the new women workers were heading, whether toward degradation or independence.

G roups of merry and somewhat loud-talking girls, whose ages might range from twelve to twenty, came by with a buoyant step. They were most of them factory girls, and wore the usual out-of-door dress of that particular class of maidens; namely, a shawl, which at midday or in fine weather was allowed to be merely a shawl, but towards evening, or if the day were chilly, became a sort of Spanish mantilla or

Scotch plaid, and was brought over the head and hung loosely down, or was pinned under the chin in no unpicturesque fashion.

"Their faces were not remarkable for beauty; indeed, they were below the average, with one or two exceptions; they had dark hair, neatly and classically arranged, dark eyes, but sallow complexions and irregular features. The only thing to strike a passer-by was an acuteness and intelligence of countenance, which has often been noticed in a manufacturing population."

The mill women thus described by Mrs. Gaskell have come to stand, in popular opinion, for the Victorian working woman. Appropriated by the social scientist as they have been, studied minutely from a variety of sources, and presented to the public with a wealth of detail in numerous important books dealing with the industrial development of nineteenth-century England, they have received the notoriety achieved by no other class of women workers. Such emphasis they have entirely merited. They have had an indissoluble connection with some of the most momentous changes to be recorded in history, and are without doubt the most important Victorian working women. . . .

In 1832 women were to be found in almost every department of the cotton factories. They beat the cotton by hand. In the carding-room they were back-frame, bobbin-frame, and drawing-tenters. They were twist-winders and stretchers. They were throstle spinners, and before they were entirely replaced by men who could watch two mules and repair their machines, they were also mule spinners. They worked at the power-looms in the weaving sheds. In the silk factories women were employed in every part of the industry, even acting as overlookers in one mill. In worsted and woolen mills young girls were spinners as well as weavers. . . .

Changed conditions in the country often turned the tide of labourers northward. The Enclosure Acts between 1700 and 1800 had already driven large numbers of the yeomanry, the country freeholders, and the labourers, formerly with a little land of their own, into the towns and into mills. Agricultural reforms, such as the reclaiming of waste lands and peat bogs once used by small-holders, and the enclosure of the commons, where the cattle and pigs had been allowed to feed, created a large class of workers entirely dependent on wages. The custom of gleaning after the harvest was also taken away. After the Industrial Revolution had killed the domestic industries which had formerly helped out the earnings of farm workers, their condition had become pitiable. The North often gave the whole family employment. With the steady decline of the old village games since Puritan times, and with no other amusements taking their places, the monotony of life in farming communities encouraged restless people to flock to the industrial towns. . . .

In the Government returns in 1834 a detailed report was made comparing the wages of men and women at different ages employed in all branches of the textile industry. In cotton in Lancashire the highest average wage for men at the age of greatest efficiency was 22s. 8½d. as compared with 9s. 8¼d. for women. In the woollen, worsted, flax, and silk mills there was a similar proportion.

To one writer, at least, such figures were a subject for congratulation. Dr. Ure writes:

"Factory females have in general much lower wages than males, and they have been pitied on this account with perhaps an injudicious sympathy, since the low price of their labour here tends to make household duties their most profitable as well as agreeable occupation, and prevents them from being tempted by the mill to abandon the care of their offspring at home. Thus Providence effects its purpose with a wisdom and efficacy which should repress the short-sighted presumption of human devices."

One wonders how this writer interpreted the conditions of 1844, when poverty and the power-loom attracted thousands of women to the mills. . . .

Fifteen and eighteen [hours of work] were frequent when trade was brisk. Again and again in the reports of the factory inspectors attention was brought to the prevalent overwork of women. They often worked at night. Charlotte Elizabeth Tonna showed from Government reports such labour continuing for several weeks.

Women were discriminated against by both their employers and the men with whom they worked. Manufacturers preferred them because they were cheap. In 1833 the owners of a Scotch mill hired women spinners at wages one-thirteenth below those of the men. Although the association of spinners prevented this reduction, eleven women at an average of 18s. weekly and one woman, working a greater number of spindles, at 30s., were retained by the company in spite of the efforts of the men. But their threats kept seven women from work, and crowds of seven or eight thousand, throwing stones and shouting after the insistent women, forced one of the partners to accompany them to work and to give them temporary living-quarters within the walls of the mill. Agnes Robertson, a widow thirty-four years old with four children, was one of the spinners employed. She testified that she was knocked about by the mob crowded around her house, so that she could not get in or out of it. They broke the windows and kept up such tumult at night that she could not sleep. Her piecer was seized by the men and beaten, and the mob trampled on her feet. When the firm finally advertised the fact that women would be paid the same wages as men, the rioting ceased. Manufacturers also found women more docile to manage. They were not restricted by the regulations of a labour union, and could be used to break strikes. They did not dispute the orders of the overlookers as did the men. They would work at night when men insisted on a decent season of rest.

All women were regarded in the first half of the nineteenth century solely as potential mothers. The worker with her own earnings was, accordingly, an affront against nature and the protective instincts of man. That the family was affected by the labour of girls and women in the mills was a consideration that roused general concern. The question of the health of human beings who were entrusted with the responsibility of the next generation, the conflict of factory work and long hours with domestic life and with a mother's care of her home and her children, the moral and spiritual degradation which might result from the employment of females outside their homes — with all this most of the literature dealing with the new industrial age was primarily concerned.

Concerning the health of mill women there was great divergence of opinion. One group contended that excessive labour where the temperature ranged from 84 to 90 degrees in the cotton-spinning department, and to 120 and 140 degrees in the linen mills, where the air was vitiated by the fluff in the carding-room and dust in the picking-room of cotton mills, and the workers wet to the waist, in the wet-spinning process of flax, stood in bare feet on the wet floor in a steamy atmosphere, was a menace to health. Poor ventilation was common. The older mills had too few windows. Those of the improved mills were often kept closed. In the usual airless workroom the smell of oil and gases further vitiated the atmosphere. The noise of machinery, which modern ingenuity has not yet conquered, added to the discomfort. All of the work was done standing, and piecers, according to the calculations given by Lord Ashley to Parliament, travelled from seventeen to twenty-seven miles, with the additional strain of turning the body round to the reverse direction four or five thousand times in a day. Meal-times before 1844 and later were often crowded out by the practice of cleaning the machinery at noon or by a rush of extra work. Food standing in the workroom and covered with fluff was eaten hurriedly, the workers often snatching a bit of it when they could. There were no proper rooms for washing, dressing, or eating. Toilet facilities were inadequate. In many departments women worked where they had no protection from machinery, and their long hair and loose aprons exposed them more than the men. One girl who was caught by the clothes in a shaft revolving at great speed was given one hundred pounds damages when ten shillings would have paid for the enclosing of the machinery. Women were scalped, arms and fingers were crushed, and legs were wounded by unboxed machinery.

The new girl of 1832 caused many a headshake. She was dangerously independent because she had her own money. Even a wife began to adopt grand airs unbefitting her position. Although her husband was entitled legally to her wages and could get drunk on them while she and her children went without food, as Barbara Bodichon pointed out, still she often found a way of asserting her right to the money she had earned. But no writer of the period found anything but evil in the downfall of the old feudal family system. In these strange new ways the critics of the factory saw fresh evidence to support them in their position that women ought to be kept out of the mills. That both wives and daughters had worked even harder when they assisted the hand-loom weavers at home, without the satisfaction of an independent wage, was never suggested. Equally unthinkable was the possibility that a daughter of mature age had the right to spend her earnings as she pleased, if she paid for her board at home, or that lodgings for a working girl gave her a splendid independence. The economically independent wife who was a benefit to society because she was free, not a slave, was a figure of the future. The family has been covered with so much sentiment that even the twentieth century has not been able to show what a harmful and dangerous institution it can be. The Victorians must accordingly be excused for their blindness to its faults.

The popular opinion of the factory girl was that her morals were very bad, if we judge from the literature on the subject. Her degradation was traced, directly or indirectly, to her employment outside the home. . . . A general looseness in morals was proved by the number of illegitimate children born to girls in certain mills. An examination of the figures, however, indicates that they could be matched in any agricultural district, and surpassed among servants, as the Government records themselves proved. But at the same time that immorality was being computed according to offspring born out of wedlock, the charge was made that the fact that no more unlawful children could be produced for the records was attributable to the wide circulation of books on birth control by Richard Carlile. Under such disadvantages any accurate information about morals is not obtainable. Too much of the material is like that of Engels, a rough estimate that three-fourths of the factory hands between fourteen and twenty were unchaste, something impossible to prove. The opinions of midwives, of factory girls and their parents, of husbands, of employers, all result in a conflict of evidence that leads nowhere. Along with this sexual laxity went such vices as theft, smoking, drinking, swearing, and filthy language. The drinking was given special emphasis by the figures of a borough-reeve of Manchester, who counted the number of people entering a certain gin-shop in five minutes during eight successive Saturday nights and at different periods in the evening. . . . Women were accused of using drugs as well as men. Pawnshops were frequently used by improvident work-people. Girls bought luxuries in dress on credit, and escaped debt and imprisonment by moving from place to place. . . .

Joan W. Scott and Louise A. Tilly

WOMEN'S WORK AND THE FAMILY IN 19TH CENTURY EUROPE

This recent study by two American historians shifts the focus away from just factory work to continuities in older forms of women's labor

Joan W. Scott & Louise A. Tilly, "Women's Work and the Family in 19th Century Europe," pp. 40-43; 44-45; 52-53; 54; 61-63. Copyright © *Comparative Studies in Society and History*, Volume 17#1 (Jan, 1975). Cambridge University Press, New York.

and of values that associated work and family. But it notes the new profile of women workers in the most industrial countries; continuities could certainly be overwhelmed by change. The selection is vitally concerned with values, which is another version of the big problem of culture vs. behavior. Even when women did new *forms* of work, had their motivation and expectations changed? And if not, was there in fact much change at all from the standpoint of women themselves; a revolutionary economy amid an almost changeless womankind? Was even serious evolution delayed, conditioned still in the twentieth century by contact (a comfort or an inhibition) with the past? These are key questions around the issue of whether modern women were becoming liberated (and from what) and/or adapting with surprising ease to an undeniably new economy and/or left behind as men seized the really important positions.

W hen census figures finally provide marital status, some big national differences can be noted. In 1911, while 69 percent of all single women in Britain worked, only 9.6 percent of married women did. In France in 1896, 52 percent of all single women were in the labor force, and 38 percent of married women. Although our evidence is impressionistic and scattered, it looks as though as industrialization advanced (at least in the pre-1914 period), fewer married women worked. Thus Britain, the more advanced industrial country in 1911, had the lower proportion of married women workers; on the other hand, in France, in which both agriculture and manufacturing were organized on a smaller scale than in Britain, more married women were in the labor force.

Why did women work in the nineteenth century and why was the female labor force predominantly young and single? To answer these questions we must first examine the relationship of these women to their families of origin (the families into which they were born), not to their families of procreation (the family launched at marriage). We must ask not only how husbands regarded their wives' roles, but what prompted families to send their *daughters* out into the job market as garment workers or domestic servants.

The parents of these young women workers during industrialization were mostly peasants and, to a lesser extent, urban workers. When we examine the geographic and social origins of domestic servants, one of the largest groups of women workers, their rural origins are clear. Two-thirds of all the domestic servants in England in 1851 were daughters of rural laborers. . . .

The hierarchical division of labor within the family, which assigned the husband the role of breadwinner and the wife the role of domestic manager and moral guardian, emerged clearly only in the nineteenth century and was associated with the growth of the middle class and the diffusion of its values. On the other hand, as we will demonstrate at length below, traditional ideas about women held by peasant and laboring families did not find feminine and economic functions incompatible. In the pre-industrial Europe described by Peter Laslett and in contemporary pre-modern societies studied by anthropologists, the household or the family is the crucial economic unit. Whether or not all work is done at home, all family members are expected to work. It is simply assumed that women will work, for their contribution is valued as necessary for the survival of the family unit. The poor, the illiterate, the economically and politically powerless of the past operated according to values which fully justified the employment of women outside the home.

We are arguing then, . . . that pre-industrial values, rather than a new individualistic ideology, justified the work of working-class women in the nineteenth century. . . . We also reject the . . . argument which says that material changes in economic, political or social structures led directly and immediately to changes in values and behavior. It, too, is based on a model which assumes that change in one realm necessarily and directly leads to change in another. Thus Engels tells us that the coming of capitalism excluded women from 'participation in social production' and reduced their role and status to that of servants in the home. Proletarian women are exceptions to this description because in industrial society they are engaged in social production. Nonetheless, in both instances, Engels makes a direct connection between economic change and changes in values and status.

Our examination of the evidence on women's work in the nineteenth century has led us to a different understanding of the process which led to the relatively high employment of women outside the home in nineteenth-century Europe. The model we use posits a continuity of traditional values and behavior in changing circumstances. Old values coexist with and are used by people to adapt to extensive structural changes. This assumes that people perceive and act on the changes they experience in terms of ideas and attitudes that they already hold. ... Behavior is less the product of new ideas than of the effects of old ideas operating in new or changing contexts.

Traditional families then, operating on long-held values, sent their daughters to take advantage of increased opportunities generated by industrialization and urbanization. Industrial development did not affect all areas of a given country at the same time. Rather the process can best be illustrated by an image of 'islands of development' within an underdeveloped sea, islands which drew population to them from the less developed areas. The values of the less developed sector were imported into the developing sector and there were extended, adapted and only gradually transformed.

As peasant values were imported, so was the behavior they directed. And work for the wives and daughters of the poor was a familiar experience in pre-industrial societies. No change in values, then, was necessary to permit lower class women to work outside the home during the nineteenth century. Neither did industrialization 'emancipate' these women by permitting more of them to work outside the home. And, given the fluctuations in the size of the female labor force especially, it is difficult to see any direct connection between the work of peasant and working-class women and the political enfranchisement of all women.

Let us now attempt to reconstruct the historical experience of women workers during the early stages of industrialization. Since most were of rural origin, we will begin by examining the peasant or family economy whose values and economic needs sent them into the job market.

Commentators on many different areas of Europe offer strikingly similar descriptions of peasant social organization. Anthropologists and social historians seem to agree that regardless of country 'the peasantry is a pre-industrial social entity which carries over into contemporary society specific elements of a different, older, social structure, economy and culture.' The crucial unit of organization is the family 'whose solidarity provides the basic framework for mutual aid, control and socialization'. The family's work is usually directed to the family farm, property considered to belong to the group rather than to a single individual. 'The individual, the family and the farm appear as an indivisible whole'. 'Peasant property is, at least *de facto*, family property. The head of the family appears as the manager rather than the proprietor of family land.' ...

Members of the family or household have clearly defined duties, based in part on their age and their position in the family and in part on their sex. Sex role differentiation clearly existed in these societies. Men and women not only performed different tasks, but they occupied different space. Most often, although by no means always, men worked the fields while women managed the house, raised and cared for animals, tended a garden and marketed surplus dairy products, poultry and vegetables. There was also seasonal work in the fields at planting and harvest times. ...

Long before the nineteenth century, lower-class families had sent their daughters out to work. The continuation of this practice and of the values and assumptions underlying it is evident not only in the fact of large numbers of single women working but also in the age structure of the female labor force, in the kinds of work these women did and in their personal behavior.

The fact that European female labor forces consisted primarily of young, single women — girls, in the language of their contemporaries — is itself an indication of the persistence of familial values. Daughters were expendable in rural and urban households, certainly more expendable than their mothers and, depending on the work of the family, their brothers. When work had to be done away from home and when its duration was uncertain, the family interest was best served by sending forth its daughters. Domestic service, the chief resort of most rural girls, was a traditional area of employment. It was often a secure form of migration since a young girl was assured a place to live, food, and a family. There were risks involved also; servant unemployment and servant exploitation were real. Nevertheless, during the nineteenth century, though many more girls were sent into service and moved farther from home than had traditionally been the case, the move itself was not unprecedented. Domestic service was an acceptable employment partly because it afforded the protection of a family and membership in a household.

This was true not only of domestic service, but of other forms of female employment. In Italy and France, textile factory owners attempted to provide "family" conditions for their girls. Rules of conduct limited their activity, and nuns supervised the establishments, acting as substitute parents. *In loco parentis* for some factory owners sometimes even meant arranging suitable marriages for their female operatives. These factory practices served the owner's interests too, by keeping his work force under control and limiting its mobility. They also served the interests of the girls' families more than those of the girls as individuals, for the girls'

wages sometimes went directly to their parents. We do not wish to argue that the factory dormitory was a beneficent institution. The fact that it used the family as model for work and social relationships, and the fact that the practice did serve the *family* interest to some degree, is, however, important. . . .

Domestic service, garment-making and even textile manufacturing, the three areas in which female labor was overwhelmingly concentrated, were all traditional areas of women's work. The kind of work parents sent their daughters to do, in other words, did not involve a radical departure from the past. Many a wife had spent her girlhood in service at someone else's house. Piece-work and spinning and weaving were also common in traditional households. The *location* of work did change and that change eventually led to a whole series of other differences: but, initially, there must have been some comfort for a family sending a daughter to a far-off city in the fact that they were sending her to do familiar, woman's work.

As parents sent daughters off with traditional expectations, so the daughters attempted to fulfill them. Evidence for the persistence of familial values is found in the continuing contributions made by working daughters to their families. If in some cases factories sent the girls' wages to their parents, in others, girls simply sent most of their money home themselves. In England, it was not until the 1890s that single working girls living at home kept some of their own money. Earlier, on the continent, their counterparts 'normally turned over all their pay to the family fund'. The daughter of a Belgian locksmith first served her family by tailoring. She habitually gave her family all her earnings 'and thus had no savings at the time of her marriage'. Irish migrants sent money back from as far away as London and Boston. And, even when they no longer expected to return home to marry and live in their natal villages, French and Italian servant girls continued to send money back home. . . .

Traditional values did not persist indefinitely in modern or modernizing contexts.

As families adapted customary strategies to deal with new situations they became involved in new experiences which altered relationships within the family and the perceptions of those relationships. As the process of change involved retention of old values and practices, it also transformed them, but in a . . . gradual and complex manner. . . .

The major transformation involved the replacement of familial values with individualistic ones. These stressed the notion that the individual was owner of him- or herself rather than a part of a social or moral whole. They involved what Anderson calls 'an instrumental orientation' of family members to their families 'requiring reciprocation for their contribution in the very short run'. These attitudes developed differently in different places depending in part on specific circumstances. Nonetheless, the evidence indicates an underlying similarity in the process and the final outcome. Sons first, and only later daughters, were permitted to keep some of their earnings. They were granted allowances by their parents in some cases; in others a specified family contribution was set, to still others the child decided what portion of her pay she would send home (and it diminished and became increasingly irregular over time). Anderson points out that in Preston [Lancashire], high factory wages of children reversed normal dependencies and made parents dependent on their children. The tensions created by the different priorities of parents and children led to feuds. And in these situations children often left home voluntarily and gladly and 'became unrestrained masters of their destiny'.

Long distance and permanent migration also ultimately undermined family ties. And the pressures of low wages and permanent urban living, the forced independence of large numbers of young girls, clearly fostered calculating, self-seeking attitudes among them. They began to look upon certain jobs as avenues of social and occupational mobility, rather than as a temporary means to earn some money for the family. Domestic service remained a major occupation for women until the twentieth century in most of Europe. (In fact, in the mid-nineteenth century the number of women employed as domestics increased tremendously.) Nonetheless, as it embodied traditional female employment, a position as a servant also began to mean an opportunity for geographic and occupational mobility. Once the trip to the city and the period of adjustment to urban life had been accomplished under the auspices of service, a young girl could seek better and more remunerative work. Her prospects for marrying someone who made better money in the city also increased immeasurably.

Their new experiences and the difficulties and disillusionment they experienced clearly developed in young women a more individualistic and instrumental orientation. They lived and worked with peers increasingly. They wanted to save their money for clothes and amusements. They learned to look out for their own advantage, to value every penny they earned, to place their own desires and interests above those of their families.

Decreased infant mortality and increased educational opportunity also modified family work strategies. And instead of sending all their children out to work for the family welfare, parents began to invest in their children's futures by keeping them out of the work force and sending them to school. (Clearly this strategy was adopted earlier for sons than daughters — the exact history of the process remains to be described.) The family ethic at once sponsored intergenerational mobility and a new individualistic attitude as well.

A number of factors, then, were involved in the waning of the family economy. They included the location of job opportunities, increased standards of living and higher wages, proximity to economic change, increased exposure to and adherence to bourgeois standards as chances for mobility into the bourgeoisie increased, ethnic variations in work patterns and family organization, and different rates of development in different regions and different countries. All of these factors contributed to the decline of the family as a productive unit and to the modification of the values associated with it.

The decline can be dated variously for various places, classes and ethnic groups. It reached the European peasant and working classes only during the nineteenth century, and in some areas, like Southern Italy, rural Ireland and rural France, not until the twentieth century. The usefulness of the family model as a unit of analysis for social relationships and economic decision making, however, has not disappeared.

A great deal more work is needed on the redefinition of family relationships and on the changes in the definition of women's work and women's place that accompanied it. Clearly many things changed. The rising standard of living and increased wages for men, which enabled them to support their families, made it less necessary for married women to work outside the home. (In early industrialization, such work also exacted great costs in terms of infant and child mortality.) Even for single women, economic change reduced traditional work opportunities, while new jobs opened up for those with more education. After World War I, for example, domestic service was much less important as an area of employment for young women. A smaller number of permanent servants who followed that occupation as a profession replaced the steady stream of young women who had constituted the domestic servant population. The rise of factory garment production seems to have limited work available for women in Milan and elsewhere. On the other hand, the growth of new jobs in expanding government services, in support services for business, in commerce, in health services and in teaching provided work opportunities, primarily for single women, especially for those with at least a basic education.

III. THE FAMILY AND VICTORIAN CULTURE

Bernard I. Murstein

LOVE, SEX AND MARRIAGE THROUGH THE AGES

In work historians of women long found change and now tend to see continuity; in family continuity has traditionally been stressed — old values given new importance — with change only more recently coming to the fore. This results in part from an effort to deal with the whole of women's lives, relating work and family to each other; culture or values linking family to other activities here form a vital bridge. But this statement does not remove problems of interpretation, for the family as a Victorian cultural artifact applies in the first instance to the middle classes, whose women were not employed; and the challengers of the conventional view in this area are stressing new behavior against publicly touted standards of respectability, finding a new culture growing up primarily among those women who did not hold jobs and almost unconsciously beneath the rhetoric of Victorian respectability. At an extreme, it is argued that the real revolution did not occur at first in work at all, for women workers were locked in the most traditional and pervasive family culture, but within precisely those middle-class homes that have long seemed so stultified.

First, though, consider the conventional view that sees Victorian family culture as widespread, perhaps even uniting various social classes in their view of the proper situation for adult women. The picture can be generally agreed upon, for disputes involve mainly the extent of its applicability to real life, but one important feature must be noted. Most people who comment on Victorian women regard their family life as a strange and rather repulsive museum piece; official Victorian culture has few defenders among women's historians. But insofar as it is strange, then a key change must have occurred since; when, and why? And against the notion that it is repulsive, note the widespread current lament that the family is decaying, a lament not applied primarily to the situation of women so much as to the family as a whole but which suggests that perhaps the Victorian family, if it existed as official culture said it did, was not so repulsive after all? Again, the question is by what standards we judge.

Bernard Murstein, a psychologist and expert on sex, here relying on literary and philosophical sources, sums up a number of common impressions in a brief survey of Victorian marriage and the particular role of women in it. Nancy Cott, a historian, uses more clearly the kind of cultural sources that produce this view of the family in her study of women in early nineteenth-century New England. She also asserts the novelty of the Victorian family ethic and seeks its causes. In so doing she may suggest that the ethic was not so damaging to women as its bald presentation can imply, or at least that there are no unqualified villains involved.

Keats exclaimed, "God! she is like a milk-white lamb that bleats for man's protection." Michelet lamented the pain, languor, and weakness endured by this poor creature because of menstruation. This "cicatrization of an interior wound [resulted in the fact that] 15 or 20 days out of 28 (we may say nearly always) woman is not only an invalid, but a wounded one." Comte saw femininity as a kind of prolonged infancy, and Balzac felt that women were incapable of reason or of absorbing useful knowledge from books. Hegel considered women capable of education in the lower arts but certainly not in the advanced sciences, in philosophy, or even some art forms. He explained:

The difference between men and women is like that between animals and plants. Men correspond to animals, while women correspond to plants because their development is more placid and the principle that underlies it is the rather vague unity of feeling. When women hold the helm of government, the state is at once in jeopardy, because women regulate their actions not by the demands of university but by arbitrary inclinations and opinions. Women are educated – who knows how? – as it were by breathing in ideas, by living rather than by acquiring knowledge. The status of manhood, on the other hand, is attained only by the stress of thought and much technical exertion.

Another German philosopher, Arthur Schopenhauer, saw woman as more advanced along the phylogenetic scale. She was definitely of the order Homo sapiens – somewhere between a child and a full-grown man. Concerning her specific characteristics, he was less kind:

The only business that really claims their earnest attention is love, making conquests, and everything connected with this – dress, dancing, and so on . . . the fundamental fault of the female character is

that it has *no sense of justice* . . . a woman who is perfectly truthful and not given to dissimulation is perhaps an impossibility. . . . It is only the man whose intellect is clouded by his sexual impulses that could give the name of *the fair sex* to that undersized, narrow-shouldered, broad-hipped, and short-legged race. . . . The sympathies that exist between them and men are skin-deep only, and do not touch the mind or the feelings or the character.

Years later, Charles Darwin was to put evolution on the side of male supremacy when he noted that, through sexual selection, "the chief distinction in the intellectual powers of the two sexes is shewn by man's attaining to a higher eminence, in whatever he takes up, than can woman. . . . Thus man has ultimately become superior to woman."

Another group of men did not so much emphasize woman's inferiority as her natural goodness: she was meek, gentle, soft, and submissive. In *War and Peace* she was Nicholas' wife, and Nicholas could only "wonder at her spirituality and at the lofty moral world, almost beyond his reach." Ruskin, "she must be enduringly, incorruptibly good; instinctively, unfailibly wise – wise, not for self-development, but for self-renunciation."

All these virtues were already embodied in the stereotype of the good German housewife who rarely went out and centered all her attention on the family circle. Her three functions in life have become a stereotype: Kinder, Küche, Kirche.

It is noteworthy that Anton Chekhov, the brilliant Russian writer, saw through the caricature of women that men were creating. He wrote in his notebook, "to demand that the woman one loves should be pure is egotistical: to look for that in a woman which I have not got myself is not love, but worship, since one ought to love one's equal. . . ."

Victorian husband-wife relationships represented a triumph of role stereotype over reality. Women were gaining increasing competence in the social and educational spheres: yet they were asked to play a role which demanded complete subordination of their selves to the ego of their husbands. The roles were so clear that a random sample of European works shows the basic essentials of this stereotype. Tolstoy's *War and Peace* describes Pierre as having the right to regulate the whole family in accordance with his wishes. *A Doll's House*, by Ibsen, deals with the treatment of a woman as a child-wife by her patronizing husband. "How warm and cosy our home is, Nora," he tells her. "Here is shelter for you; here I will protect you like a hunted dove that I have saved from a hawk's claws! I will bring peace to your poor beating heart." Balzac declares that a husband must be imposing and a despot, whereas "a wife is what her husband makes her."

The female retort — for example, in Sara Ellis' *The Wives of England* — was feeble. She noted that husbands are selfish; but instead of blaming them, the ladies should pity them, for the selfish are never happy. In a similar vein, women are superior to men, who — unlike women — lack empathy or the ability to put themselves in other people's shoes. But the fact that women were more sensitive than men was small consolation. The morally superior were trapped in a tightly prescribed code of behavior, and less virtuous men were expected to transgress against the virtuous from time to time — otherwise they would not be morally inferior!

As a sexless creature, a woman might pity her suitor or husband because he suffers from the sting of lust; she might be grateful for his affection, and she would of course love him as a duty — but she would not *respond.* In the words of Dr. Gregory, even if the woman did love her suitor, "never dis-cover to him the full extent of your love, no, not although you marry him. That sufficiently shows your preference, which is all he is entitled to know."

That the ladies allowed themselves to be forced into this narrow concept of femininity is apparent from magazine comments such as those in the *Quarterly Review*, which lamented that "the more admirable the wives [i.e., the more they fitted the ideal stereotype] the more profoundly bored the husbands." For such bored husbands, prostitutes proved eminently more attractive. A commentary on the times appeared in de Maupassant's story "Au bord du lit"; in it, the husband, to gain some measure of sexual happiness, pays his wife a sum of money to ensure a good sexual performance.

One of the first quantitative surveys on marital happiness was conducted by Gross Hoffinger in Germany in 1847. Of the 100 marriages surveyed, he found 48 couples distinctly unhappy, 36 indifferent to each other but managing to live together, 15 happy, and 1 "virtuous." He placed the responsibility for this sad state of affairs at the doorstep of the men, as opposed to the women, by a ratio of 2.5 to 1.

In a few rare cases, drastic measures could be taken to alleviate marital unhappiness. A folkloric notion existed in England that by putting a wife up for auction (with her permission), the marital ties could be legally snapped. Accordingly, in 1832 a farmer, Joseph Thomson, put his 22-year-old wife on the block, with her consent, for the sum of 50 shillings. The price proved unrealistic, so he finally disposed of her for 20 shillings and a Newfoundland dog.

The possibility that the cause of discord might be the social, political, and legal inequality of the sexes did not at first win much support. Instead, male brutality, drunkenness, or insensitivity was generally blamed. *Fraser's Magazine,* calling for kindness toward women, saw a typical marital quarrel in the following vein: "Imagine the offender a well-dressed gentlemen, tall and powerful . . . the victim shrinking from his blows — a gentle high-bred English *lady.* Great God! Does not the picture make every true man set his teeth and clench his hand?"

In sum, we may say that the Victorian period did not offer a particularly distinguished model of connubial felicity despite its posturing of domestic joy. Victorians, however, no longer regarded marriage as simply an economic arrangement or a means of populating the world. In paying more attention to the quality of the relationship, it was natural that treatises on scientific matchmaking should come to be written.

Nancy Cott

THE BONDS OF WOMANHOOD

The central convention of domesticity was the contrast between the home and the world. Home was an "oasis in the desert," a "sanctuary" where "sympathy, honor, virtue are assembled," where "disinterested love is ready to sacrifice everything at the altar of affection." In his 1827 address on female education a New Hampshire pastor proclaimed that "It is at home, where man . . . seeks a refuge from the vexations and embarrassments of business, an enchanting repose from exertion, a relaxation from care by the interchange of affection: where some of his finest sympathies, tastes, and moral and religious feelings are formed and nourished; — where is the treasury of pure disinterested love, such as is seldom found in the busy walks of a selfish and calculating world." The ways of the world, in contrast, subjected the individual to "a desolation of feeling," in the words of the *Ladies' Magazine*; there "we behold every principle of justice and honor, and even the dictates of common honesty disregard, and the delicacy of our moral sense is wounded; we see the general good, sacrificed to the advancement of personal interest, and we turn from such scenes, with a painful sensation. . . ."

The contradistinction of home to world had roots in religious motives and rhetoric. Christians for centuries had depreciated "the world" of earthly delights and material possessions in comparison to Heaven, the eternal blessings of true faith. In the 1780s and 1790s British Evangelicals doubled the pejorative connotation of "the world," by preferring bourgeois respectability above the "gay world" of aristocratic fashion. Living in an era of eroding public orthodoxy, they considered family transmission of piety more essential than ever to the maintenance of religion; consequently they conflated the contrasts of Heaven versus "the world" and bourgeois virtue versus the "gay world" with the contrast between the domestic fireside and the world outside. In that tradition, when Esther Grout wrote in her diary, "oh how sweet is retirement. The pleasantest & I think some of the most profitable moments of my life have been spent in retirement," she was referring to her withdrawal from the world in solitary religious devotion and *also* to her repose *at home.*

The rhetorical origins of the contrast between home and world demand less interpretation than the canon of domesticity built upon it. That contrast infused the new literature because, in simplest terms, it seemed to explain and justify material change in individual's lives. Between the Revolution and the 1830s New England's population became more dense and more mobile, its political system more representative and demanding of citizens, its social structure more differentiated and its economic structure more complex than in earlier years when the business of "the world" had mostly taken place in households. Economic growth and rationalization and the entry of the market mechanism into virtually all relations of production fostered specialized and standardized work and a commercial ethic. Because of regional division of production and marketing, agricultural production itself became more specialized and more speculative. The farmer's success was not in his own hands when he produced for distant markets. In handicrafts the functional differentiation of wholesale merchant, retail merchant, contractor or "boss," and pieceworker replaced the unified eighteenth-century pattern in which an artisan made and sold his wares from his residence. Masters (now employers) and their journeymen or apprentices no longer assumed a patriarchal relationship; wages and prices defined their relationship to one another and to the merchants above them. Trends such as the decline of traditional determinants of deference, the assertion of an individualist ethos, increasing extremes of wealth and poverty, and replacement of unitary association networks by pluralistic ones, indicated deep change in social relations. Differentiation and specialization characterized this transformation of society. These were portrayed and symbolized most powerfully in the separation of production and exchange from the domestic arena — the division between "world" and "home."

The canon of domesticity encouraged people to assimilate such change by linking it to a specific set of sex-roles. In the canon of domesticity, the home contrasted to the restless and competitive world because its "presiding spirit" was woman, who was "removed from the arena of pecuniary excitement and ambitious competition." Woman inhabited the "shady green lanes of domestic life," where she found "pure enjoyment and hallowed sympathies" in her "peaceful offices." If man was the "fiercest warrior, or the most unrelenting votary of stern ambition," "toil-worn" by "troubled

scenes of life," woman would "scatter roses among the thorns of his appointed track." In the "chaste, disinterested circle of the fireside" only — that is, in the hearts and minds of sisters, wives, and mothers — could men find "reciprocated humanity ... unmixed with hate or the cunning of deceit." The spirit of business and public life thus appeared to diverge from that of the home chiefly because the two spheres were the separate domains of the two sexes.

In accentuating the split between "work" and "home" and proposing the latter as a place of salvation, the canon of domesticity tacitly acknowledged the capacity of modern work to desecrate the human spirit. Authors of domestic literature, especially the female authors, denigrated business and politics as arenas of selfishness, exertion, embarrassment, and degradation of soul. These rhetoricians suggested what Marx's analysis of alienated labor in the 1840s would assert, that "the worker ... feels at ease only outside work, and during work he is outside himself. He is at home when he is not working and when he is working he is not at home." The canon of domesticity embodied a protest against that advance of exploitation and pecuniary values. Nancy Sproat, a pious wife and mother who published her own family lectures in 1819, warned that "the air of the world is poisonous. You must carry an antidote with you, or the infection will prove fatal." (A latter-day Calvinist, she clearly gave "the world" dual meaning, opposing it to both "home" and "Heaven." Her antidote, likewise, was a compound, of domestic affection and religious faith.) No writer more consistently emphasized the anti-pecuniary bias of the domestic rhetoric than Sarah Josepha Hale, influential editor of the Boston *Ladies' Magazine* from 1828 to 1836 and subsequently of *Godey's Lady's Book* in Philadelphia. "Our men are sufficiently money-making," Hale said. "Let us keep our women and children from the contagion as long as possible. To do good and to communicate, should be the motto of Christians and republicans." She wished "to remind the dwellers in this 'bank-note world' that there are objects more elevated, more worthy of pursuit than wealth." "Time is money" was a maxim she rejected, and she urged mothers to teach their children the relative merits of money and of good works.

Yet the canon of domesticity did not directly challenge the modern organization of work and pursuit of wealth. Rather, it accommodated and promised to temper them. The values of domesticity undercut opposition to exploitative pecuniary standards in the work world, by upholding a "separate sphere" of comfort and compensation, instilling a morality that would en-

courage self-control, and fostering the idea that preservation of home and family sentiment was an ultimate goal. Family affection, especially maternal affection, was portrayed as the "spirit indefatigable, delighting in its task," which could pervade and "regenerate" society. Furthermore, women, through their reign in the home, were to sustain the "essential elements of moral government" to allow men to negotiate safely amid the cunning, treachery, and competition of the marketplace. If a man had to enter the heartless and debasing world, his wife at home supplied motive and reward for him, to defuse his resentment. . . .

Patricia Branca and Peter N. Stearns

MODERNIZATION OF WOMEN IN THE 19TH CENTURY

This radically new view of the nineteenth-century middle-class housewife stresses the inapplicability of the Victorian myth about the sheltered woman. Using housekeeping manuals more than literary sources Patricia Branca, an American historian, paints not a woman unable to live up to the female image so much as one working out her own image, modernizing her methods and developing a new, really pioneering belief in science and progress that could be applied widely to daily activities. If this is true, we must still ask why the conventional image developed and persisted at all. Here is a distinctive view of a quiet but profound revolution among some of the Victorian women from whom one would least expect it. Tied to the family, as Branca agrees, the changes these women explored are held to be vital precisely because they related to the basic fabric of daily life. But was a new woman really being created? Was this housewife much closer to the twentieth-century woman than the more stereotyped Victorian model?

W omen in the wealthier classes of society were not affected by such dramatic changes as their poorer sisters. They were not involved, for example, in the

increase in illegitimate births. Here, the boundary line was fairly sharp, in both city and countryside, between families that had property and those that did not. In the propertied families, a fairly traditional sexual morality still predominated. This does not mean that middle-class women may not also have experienced a rising interest in sexual enjoyment, but the process was probably more gradual. In further contrast to the lower classes, middle-class women were not drawn into new economic roles. Businessmen who set up new small factories or commercial establishments often expected active support from their wives, according to a traditional pattern. Many wives kept account books, dealt with salesmen, and performed other functions in the firm. One French industrialist told his wife how he counted on her to keep his business records: "I explained to her that I wanted to be near her continually so that she would be completely informed of all our affairs."

But there was change in the middle-class situation by the early nineteenth century. The demographic revolution clearly affected this class, for here too, even if there was no increase in the number of children born, the decline in child mortality meant that business and professional people had increasingly large families, which placed growing burdens on the middle-class mother. In part because of this, women's involvement with their husbands' business activities tended to decline. The same French businessman who praised the work of wives in his generation, claiming that "the firms which prospered most quickly were precisely those in which the wives participated most," noted that, by 1850, customs had changed and the wives of merchants stayed out of business life. The middle-class household was becoming increasingly complicated, as the standard of living rose; more and more choices had to be made about what to buy. The middle-class wife became the prime agent in the transformation of the family into a unit for consumption, making fundamental decisions about the style of life the family should adopt. Above all, the urban middle class was growing very rapidly, much faster than the population as a whole. More and more women had to learn how to fulfill the middle-class expectations of what a wife and mother should be.

Not surprisingly, the middle-class situation produced the first thorough transformation of women's values, toward something recognizably modern. The process was gradual, but this was precisely why it could take hold. Lower-class women, subjected during the transitional decades to much more profound stress through the economic and demographic changes, tended to try to recapture family traditions. They had to develop new behavior in order to do this, but it was some time before really new goals began to emerge. Middle-class women could accept change more easily. While not wealthy, they were above the borderline of subsistence, and this is probably essential for the development of modern ideas.

Toward the middle of the nineteenth century the life style of most middle-class women had become fairly clearly defined. In some respects it seems quite unmodern, although recognizable. It was home-centered: the middle-class wife had little to do with her husband's work. She was supposed to provide a secure refuge for her husband at the end of a hard day, as well as raising her children to be respectable citizens. A large literature developed, constituting a major part of Victorian culture, that told women they were expected to be pure, cultivated, and modest — an ornament in the family and the guardian of morality. And of course women remained restricted by laws that gave husbands control over property. They were taught from childhood that marriage was their appropriate role, and as girls had little experience outside the family context. At most they might go to a day school where the values of loyalty to the family would also be stressed.

And yet, once [she was] married, the middle-class wife had both need and opportunity to develop some modern values. She was aware of the culture that told her to be docile and pure and rarely defied it directly, but this did not define her whole life. In a sense the distinctiveness of her life derived from her middling position in society. As against the working class, middle-class women directed a household economy well above the subsistence level. Food was varied, with a considerable emphasis on meat. Houses or apartments had up to five rooms on the average. At the same time the middle class was not wealthy and urban life confronted middle-class women with some of the same problems that the workers had. There was a fear of overcrowding and of dirt and disease. Middle-class families moved frequently and the task of packing a complex household was awesome; it was often noted that three moves were worse than a fire. In contrast, upper-class women, even in newly-rich families, avoided some of the worst problems of urbanization by maintaining control over the better sections of the city. And many maintained or developed traditional rural ties as well, by keeping a place in the country to which they would regularly retreat. It was the upper-class woman, in fact, who could come closest to the ideal of gentility which was really an effort to resist change within the family.

Middle-class women thus had some means to respond to new opportunities, but the modernization process was to a large extent forced upon them by the pressures of urban life. A number of other factors promoted a distinctive response. The middle-class woman was literate, and by the middle of the nineteenth century a wide variety of magazines had been created to serve her. She read serialized fiction, advice to mothers and homemakers, medical manuals — indeed her reading interests helped shape the whole newspaper and magazine industry. What she read was rarely radical, but it could give her a variety of new ideas. Above all, her reading material was largely secular. Middle-class women did not defy religion, but in most countries religion lost much of its traditional hold over them during the second half of the nineteenth century. Prior to that time, women's literature had been heavily religious but now successful periodicals such as the *Englishwoman's Domestic Magazine* made it a matter of policy to refuse to answer religious questions or even to publish pious poems sent in by readers. Judging by the magazines, the condition of a woman's wash, the whiteness of her complexion, the softness of her hands had become more impor-

tant than the state of her soul.

Middle-class families probably relied less on ties with other relatives than was true of other social classes. The nuclear family unit of wife, husband and children often predominated, particularly of course when the family moved from city to city, as was true of a number of professional people and some businessmen. Thus many women lacked guidance from experienced kin, which eliminated a common link with tradition and allowed middle-class women to modernize more quickly than other sectors of society which maintained stronger traditional ties.

The actual impact of modernization on the lives of middle-class women is easier to determine than precise causes of the process, which remain to be more fully investigated. Urban industrial living took away many of the traditional functions of the woman. For example, she would no longer bake her own bread, nor churn her own butter, nor brew her own beer. City life provided her most of these services. Her increasing prosperity allowed the middle-class woman especially to partake of these new services. At the same time, the new prosperity brought with it a major responsibility for the middle-class wife: the management of the family's resources. As she escaped the burden of producing for the family, she assumed the responsibility of consuming for the family — a modern way of living. A wise observer of Victorian society noted that in the second half of the century it was the task of the English woman to expend the collective earnings of the whole English nation.

In her role as manager of the family's finances, which now assumed growing importance, the middle-class woman had to accept many modern concepts. Detailed planning and careful keeping of accounts became the norm for the middle class in running their households as in their business. In order to maintain a middle-class standard of living, which was progressive, the woman had to learn to look at her expenses and resources with a long range view. She could not live from day to day. She now had to plan her finances on a yearly basis. This was part of the new science that came to dominate middle-class household management in the second half of the century — the science of Domestic Economy. The middle-class woman was the major purchaser of the hundreds of manuals which flooded the market in the second half of the century claiming to apply the new advances in science to household affairs. Admittedly, the middle-class housewife was not always successful in running her increasingly complicated household, but she did display a willingness to accept and try new concepts.

One of the clearest illustrations of the middle-class woman's willingness to participate in the mainstream of modern society was her readiness to accept novel technology into her home. The sewing machine is just one important example of the changing behavior of the middle-class woman, as it spread widely after 1850. Objections were voiced concerning the sewing machine, similar in many ways to those raised early in the century over the introduction of machines into industry. There was the lament that the sewing machine would destroy the long-valued skill of hand sewing — that element of personal touch associated with the craft and womanhood. However, the criticism was never persuasive enough to deter the middle-class woman as she quickly adopted the new invention. No doubt the primary reason women welcomed this advance was necessity, for there were just so many hours in the day, and so much time to spend sewing.

In some respects the woman's decision to buy the sewing machine can be seen as an expression of individualism. With the sewing machine, the middle-class woman acquired a new piece of property that was hers, as well as one that worked primarily for her benefit. Viewed in the light of modernization, the familiar list of other household innovations, which expanded rapidly after mid-century, such as the washing machine and carpet sweepers, assumes a new importance. One could argue that if the middle-class woman had not been so receptive to innovation and technology, the process of modernization could not have progressed as rapidly as it did, for in the nineteenth century the middle-class woman was the only woman who both needed and could afford the advances in technology. In other words, because of her new attitudes and her decision-making power the middle-class woman emerges as a significant force in the development of a consumer goods economy.

If middle-class women were simply acquisitive beings, transforming the family into a unit of consumption, we might admit that they were becoming modern but dismiss them as rather prosaic. There were other aspects in the modernization process, however, less easy to describe but at least as significant in changing the woman's conception of herself. By the second half of the nineteenth century, middle-class women came to reject more and more the traditional fatalistic attitude toward sickness and death. By seeking advice about her health and that of her children, the middle-class woman demonstrated the belief that her world could be ordered and improved upon and was not left to be governed by some divine plan. Here again she expressed a growing reliance on science, first through her purchase of the new health manuals which were written generally by doctors to tend to her own personal health. Most important for women was the development of the special fields of gynecology and obstetrics. Obstetrics was particularly relevant, as middle-class women came to call upon the services of doctors rather than mid-wives in childbirth.

Women's expectations in health are not hard to determine, though their newness must be emphasized. They believed that doctors, being trained, would provide the latest medical advances, which would in turn reduce the chance of death for themselves and their children and curtail pain. But the medical profession did not advance as rapidly as these new middle-class expectations, and in some cases available advances were not applied because of the conservatism of most doctors. One example is the controversy which developed over the use of chloroform during childbirth. Middle-class women were trying to avoid unnecessary pain. Their response was illustrated in the story told of the first English woman to be administered chloroform during childbirth:

she was so delighted at her freedom from pain that she christened her baby Anesthesia. But doctors often objected, to some extent because they felt that a certain amount of pain was a natural part of women's life, and the use of anesthetics spread more slowly than was necessary during the nineteenth century. Women and doctors also quarreled over artificial feeding for infants. Most doctors held that breast milk was the only suitable nutrient for an infant. But middle-class women saw no reason to endure the personal discomfort and inconvenience of nursing, and quickly adopted artificial feeding as soon as glass bottles, rubber nipples, and baby formulas were developed.

Aside from housework and some new leisure activities, women's functions did not increase markedly. And here was an obvious problem: increasingly well educated and freed from frequent childbirth, the middle-class woman was faced with the problem of defining herself beyond motherhood. Here is a problem middle-class women are still coping with today, another of the tensions of modernization; but at the end of the nineteenth century it was particularly acute,

for the middle class almost never permitted its wives to work outside the home.

Middle-class women thus did not emerge triumphant from the modernization process. They had participated in great changes by 1900, in some cases setting patterns that women in other classes would later follow. But innovation could take its toll. Many people, even in the magazines widely read by women, criticized new behavior by wives and mothers. The responsibilities of running a middle-class household, where aspirations could easily outrun the money available, left many women depressed. At an extreme, heavy drinking and drug-taking — the latter relatively easy because of the use of drugs in patent medicines — affected some middle-class women. Far more women were able to adjust to modern life and to benefit by some of the changes it brought. But the problem of appropriate role remained acute: middle-class women remained for the most part tied to family and usually seemed to find this appropriate, and they had replaced some traditional functions with new ones, such as leadership in consumption of goods. But the question of fulfillment, given a new sense of individualism and the continued limitation of traditional functions, remained acute.

IV. SEXUALITY

Duncan Crow

THE VICTORIAN WOMAN

Sexual prudery is a basic feature of the Victorian stereotype. The sources for it are, again, primarily cultural, but behavior is held to have been patterned on the official ethic. Duncan Crow, a publicist who has written on a variety of popular historical subjects, gives full vent to his derision of Victorian modesty. He attempts to explain it through the conditions of the time with reference to forces of degradation near the surface of early industrial society. Does he really account for such a strange aberration that renounced the past and differs so from our enlightened selves? Who, we must wonder, were the villainous creators of the Victorian monstrosity? Here, in sum, is an interesting use of the conventional family and sexual ethic to create an almost unbelievable historical woman — could many have so repressed biological urges? (Even Crow suggests not.) Crow judges with abandon on the basis of personal convictions about what really civilized people should believe and do. A final query: if our near ancestors, the Victorians, behaved so oddly, what in fact has caused us to depart from their principles and practices? What sexual revolution has occurred and why has it occurred? Or are we in fact Victorian in our view of female sexuality still, which is why we are morbidly fascinated with accounts such as Crow's?

It is easy to despise Victorian hypocrisy, and the whole euphemistic approach that went with it, forgetting that this blinkered attitude was adopted to hide the proximity of the abyss in which seethed the primitive society the Victorians were struggling away from. It was a matter of whistling to keep up their courage. Possibly they felt that if they spoke the talisman words of hypocrisy and prudery often enough it would help to make those words come true — at least it would disguise the fact of how tenuous was their hold on this pleasanter life. To acknowledge the existence of vice, was, they believed, to encourage it. Their only defence against slipping back into the slime was, it seemed, to ignore the immorality and horrifying cruelties that surrounded them, and to adopt the canons of ultra-propriety. Any concession to tolerance or laxer living would be to lift the pawl and start the slide back to total barbarity — or at any rate it would allow the still-surrounding darkness to encroach into the drawing-room. The family was the only unit around which the defensive moat of respectability could be dug and guarded. The drawing-room was the citadel. . . .

A glorious example of the euphemistic approach that became the touchstone of Victorianism is this quotation from a book of minor morals written in the 1840s: 'The peculiar province of Woman is to tend with patient assiduity around the bed of sickness; to watch the feeble steps of infancy; to communicate to the young the elements of knowledge, and bless with their smiles those of their friends who are declining in the vale of tears.' This is not only euphemistic in language, but even more euphemistic in thought, for it is euphemistically reminding woman that it is her place to be an unintelligent, subjected soother, that and nothing more. By the time of Victoria's accession romanticism, as the essence of this quotation shows, was degenerating into anaemic sentimentalism. Added to the wealth-imposed idleness of middle-class gentility it produced the image of the ideal Victorian lady.

One notable consequence of making the drawing-room into the citadel of respectability was a fundamental change in the social attitude towards sex and its place in human relations. As part of the grand strategy for civilizing society so that it became safe for the rising middle classes it was deemed necessary to tame the savagery of sex so that it was no longer the gambolling cruel priapic anarchist that brought misrule through the carefully daubed dykes of propriety. The way to achieve this most effectively, it seemed to the collective subconscious of the "civilizers," was to ban sex as far as possible from everyday life and to enlarge to its fullest extent the interpretation of the sixth commandment so that it brought social anathema and hell-fire not only on adultery but on all lewd thoughts and fumblings.

The first step was to drive sex out of the respectable household. Admittedly if this were to be done entirely and literally the procreation of children and with it the indisputable right of the head of the household to exercise his genital instincts would be stopped, a result that would defeat the main purpose if, as was sure to happen, the roughs continued to breed without restraint and in due course, by simple weight of numbers, forcibly inherited the earth. The

solution was to apply the euphemistic approach and turn the begetting and bearing of children into an Eleusinian mystery. Ideally women would produce children by parthenogenesis; failing that, male impregnation should take place in a dark bedroom into which the husband would creep to create his offspring in silence while the wife endured the connection in a sort of coma, thereby precluding any stigma of depravity which would have been incurred by showing signs of life. Silence was important. If what went on in the dark bedroom was never mentioned, then, by a reversal of the psychological process which gives substance to a thought merely by the naming of it, sex could be dematerialized by ignoring it.

Having confined sex beneath the bedclothes by what is after all the acme of euphemism, that is by refusing to recognize its existence, another essential line of attack was to remove all other traces of it from the household. To ban it from conversation was easy enough: stern remonstrance and corporal punishment would keep the young in line. To ban it from the immediate sight was facilitated by the change in fashion which made women bell-shaped with skirts that concealed everything except the toe. Who could so much as imagine two female legs within that dome of drab material? Powerful aids as well as the pulpit, were enlisted to keep the enemy in check. Anxiety-making doctors promised disease and disintegration to those who transgressed the ascetic rules against sex. Hideous instruments were sold to prevent masturbation. And lest any thoughts of sex should be encouraged through reading books an effective censorship was exerted on novel-writers by the economically all-important circulating libraries, like Mudie's, opened in 1842, which refused to stock a book unless it eschewed the faintest suspicion of sex. Above all the embargo on sex had its anchor in the new moral attitude of the young Queen's Court which totally rejected the farmyard frankness of earlier reigns. . . .

The Early Victorians did not invent prudery, nor did they invent 'the virgin in the drawing-room,' which was what in fact, and despite her prolific offspring, they turned the Early Victorian lady into. Prudery was part of the puritan ascetic attitude to human existence and had existed since long before the nineteenth century, had existed in the Middle Ages, had existed at least since the early Christian Fathers and their Jewish predecessors. But not until economic conditions made "gentility" possible did the social climate permit the long-nurtured plants of prudery and the other repressive aspects of puritanism to burst forth and flourish in the particular colours of the age. By the time Victoria came to the throne they were coming into full flower. Similarly the virgin in the drawing-room was the re-creation in a new setting of the beneficent great mother of antiquity. . . . All this was . . . the victory in an age-old struggle for those forces which in the past had usually, except for short periods, been overborne.

The United States provided especially fertile soil. Here the plant of prudery in the 1830s was sufficiently farther forward than across the Atlantic for English visitors to remark on its profusion with wonder. Harriet Martineau in a catalogue of 'the indulgent and chivalrous treatment' that was accorded to the American woman as a substitute for justice noted that 'especially, her morals are guarded by the strictest observance of propriety in her presence'. Mrs. Trollope, too, saw and heard many examples of over-affected modesty that aroused her scorn. She had a literary conversation in Cincinnati with a gentleman, professed to be a scholar, who regarded Shakespeare as obscene, inveighed against Byron, had never heard of Ford and Massinger, and held up his hands in horror at the very title of Pope's *Rape of the Lock*. A young German gentleman told her that he had once greatly offended an important local family by saying the word 'corset' in the presence of its ladies. A signpost representing a Swiss peasant girl with her ankles showing below her petticoat caused the ladies of Cincinnati to boycott the pleasure garden where it was displayed until the petticoat was painted longer. She was told that a picnic she proposed would never come off because it was considered 'very indelicate for ladies and gentlemen to sit down together on the grass'. Nude statues were regarded as obscene spectacles, and in Philadelphia at the nineteenth annual exhibition of the Pennsylvania academy of the fine arts she found that visitors had marked and defaced 'the casts in a most indecent and shameless manner'. Men and women visited this antique statue gallery in alternate groups. . . .

Sex, of course, had not been banished from the land. Forbidden in the houses of the respectables it lost none of its strength elsewhere. If woman had been turned into the virgin in the drawing-room she had to compensate for this by being the prostitute elsewhere; and because of the extreme cosseting she received in the respectable home so the swing of ambivalence demanded that she be degraded and subject to physical brutality in her role as the hired instrument of man's pleasure outside the home. 'Thus,' says Hoffman Hays, 'the split concept, virgin and prostitute, was born.'

It is difficult to be sure why this happened. Presumably the basis of it was that male apprehensions, which had gradually become quiescent over the centuries, were somehow re-activated through the discontents of industrial society producing unbearable tensions. While the Victorian age was economically expansive and forward-looking there were strong conflicts emotionally and intellectually. Religion became an arena of passionate belief and argument as against the calm, rationalist approach of the previous century. The Bible and the security which it offered were frighteningly challenged by Darwinism and the new sciences of anthropology and psychology. There was insecurity too in the memories of the Terror during the French Revolution and these memories were reinforced by the seething workers' riots that punctuated Victoria's reign, and by the Paris Commune in 1871. In coming to power themselves the middle classes had destroyed the feudal system which kept the masses in check. Their enjoyment of prosperity and economic expansion was shot through with the nightmares of the dark in which the appalling prospect of worker domination arose. 'All of these fears and tensions,' says Hays, 'were wound in and out of the relationship between the sexes.'

All this suggests, correctly, that the 'Top Nation' Victorians felt their finger-hold on the new civilization to be so slight that it would take little to upset the whole affair and throw them back into the stews. The respectables were always conscious of the roughs lurking in the alleys. Sometimes, indeed, they emerged from the alleys into the main thoroughfares. Sir William Hardman, a mid-Victorian chronicler, mentions several of these onslaughts which were done under cover of 'rough larking'. In July 1867 he writes of 'these wretches who are the great bane of London at present, who take occasion of all bands of music, processions, and suchlike, to defy the police, knock all respectable hats over their owners' eyes, and pick all respectable pockets'. That same summer at the great Volunteer Camp at Wimbledon, 'of course the roughs (damn them) had a fine time of it, and broke through all barriers, playing havoc with the respectables'. And in November the Lord Mayor's Show was marred, as it always was, by the violence of the roughs. 'I have said for many years,' wrote Hardman, 'that the mob of roughs which this annual spectacle brought into our streets was a sight hideous and most terrible.' What was true of mid-Victorian England was even truer of the beginning of the reign when the police forces were much more rudimentary.

Nothing is so conducive to a reactionary frame of mind as the fear that one's comforts may be snatched away. Believing that human beings were still fundamentally barbarous the respectables felt the imperative need to enforce rigid tenets of behaviour without which violence and the rule of the roughs would again become supreme. And by the beginning of Victoria's reign there were plenty of people who were anxious to avoid that catastrophe: the merchants and tradesmen, and the growing professional class which was itself largely called into being by the new society. Nor was it only because they were fearful of losing their physical possessions. It was also because they were unwilling to lose the opportunity to gain and use knowledge which this new society gave them. Primitive societies had no need of engineers, nor did they give opportunities to scientists. Primitive societies destroyed Priestley's instruments. New societies watched Faraday's experiments.

Edward Shorter

THE MAKING OF THE MODERN FAMILY

Against the conventional view, two recent works appeared in the burgeoning field of the history of female sexuality, both by North American historians. Edward Shorter accepts some of the Victorian stereotype for middle-class women but says that the lower class not only ignored the official ethic but built a radical new ethic of their own that would ultimately triumph in the middle class as well, creating the fully modern woman. Victorianism is insignificant as against the nineteenth-century revolution in female sexuality. Shorter builds primarily on data on illegitimacy and the birth rate of married women, but he interprets these quite freely. Others have accepted his data but asserted that no new female spirit produced new behavior but rather a new exploitation of women's bodies by lustful men (Duncan Crow might even accept this). Agreement with Shorter thus involves assessment of some major speculative leaps, beyond exact statistics, indeed beyond the history of sex into the basic mentality and possible personal emancipation of nineteenth-century women in work as well as family relationships.

For Shorter, ultimately, the late eighteenth and the nineteenth centuries created a modern female sexual mentality while producing a distinctive demographic phase, neither traditional nor modern, with women the main agents in its development. Only birth control, dissociating sex and babies, completed the sexual modernization of women, while at the same time establishing contemporary demographic patterns.

T he central fact in the history of courtship over the last two centuries has been the enormous increase in sexual activity before marriage. Before 1800 it was unlikely that the typical young woman would have coitus with her partner — certainly not before an engagement had been sealed, and probably not as a fiancée, either. But after 1800 the percentage of young women who slept with their boyfriends or fiancés rose steadily, until in our own times it has become a majority. And recently there have been large increases especially among adolescents, in intercourse by *un*engaged women (if one can imagine such a thing).

Illegitimate births and premarital pregnancies give us the most reliable date for determining the incidence of sex before marriage. Of course, not all women who are sexually active before marriage bear children. Some practise contraception — at least to the extent of saying, as in France's Vendée, "Look out!" before their partners ejaculate. Others force an abortion or miscarry spontaneously, and still others are not yet entirely fecund. But assuming such factors remain more or less equal, there will be at least a general coincidence between the level of coitus among unmarried women and the rate at which they become pregnant. Provided that the other "intervening" variables (such as contraception) remain unchanged, we should be able to infer from a long-term rise in premarital conceptions a similar rise in sexual activity before marriage.

1550–1650. A brief, relatively insignificant rise and fall in out-of-wedlock pregnancies took place, most likely caused by a similar rise and fall in premarital intercourse. Of all periods, this is the most poorly documented; exactly what was going on in the *vie intime* of young Europeans in the late sixteenth century remains largely a mystery. Various charts of illegitimacy show an unmistakable peak in the 1590s, especially in England. Evidence is present that premarital pregnancy underwent the same uphill-downhill course. There is nothing to indicate that more sexual intercourse caused this increase. We have neither qualitative testimonies (other than the usual lamentations that the young were becoming more "immoral") nor sufficient data on such "intervening" variables as fetal mortality or female health (fecundability) to let us point to intercourse by process of elimination. As for the years that followed, the notion of the Counter-reformed, Puritanical seventeenth century as a time of sexual repression is so firmly entrenched that I shall give it a respectful nod here as the probable explanation for the charted decline between 1600 and 1650.

1750–1850. There was an enormous rise in illegitimacy and premarital pregnancy

in the years of the French and Industrial
revolutions. Late in the eighteenth century,
the number of out-of-wedlock pregnancies
began to skyrocket in virtually every community we know about, often reaching three
or four times the previous levels. In case
after case, from interior Massachusetts to the
Alpine uplands of Oberbayern, the number
of infants conceived before marriage increased markedly. Indeed this is one of the
central phenomena of modern demographic
history. In a moment I shall suggest that this
huge upsurge in part reflected a decline in
abortion and an improvement in female
health and hence reproductive biology. Primarily, however, it was the result of
increasing sexual activity. . . .

I prefer to see the giant rise in out-of-
wedlock pregnancy in the late eighteenth
century as the principal phenomenon to be
explained. It changed the lives of more
people than any fluctuation in premarital
sex had previously or has since (before the
1960s, at least). And it accords perfectly
with a larger notion of social change that I
am advancing here: that there was, once
upon a time, such a thing as traditional
society, which endured relatively unaltered
for a number of centuries but which was
finally destroyed and replaced by something
else we call "modern society." I see our own
dear modern times as entirely different from
this world we have lost, especially in everything touching intimate life, and I believe
this huge one-time change in premarital
sexual behavior to be part of the transition
from one to the other. . . .

In point of fact, the years 1750–1850
witnessed a crescendo of complaints about
immoral sexual activity among the young.
This amount of lamentation was unprecedented since the Reformation — before that
time my knowledge falters — and it was not
again to be attained until the 1920s. Doctor
after sober doctor, senior administrator
upon administrator, would turn from their
normal weighty concerns about infant hy-
giene or local self-government to comment
upon the sad state of sexual morality. What
could have been going on in their minds?
Had all these observers been seized by some

collective delusion, some secular millenarian-
ism dormant since the fifteenth century? Or
were they in fact picking up, even in their
self-inflated, self-righteous ways, a shift in
the fabric of intimate life about them? I
believe the second.

Observe some German examples. Bavari-
an administrators early in the nineteenth
century became alarmed about dancing because they thought the walk home customarily meant a stopover for sexual intercourse. Women would appear unescorted at
dance locales and wait there until they had
been asked to dance or had found a male
partner to escort them home; nine months
later the fruits of these casual couplings
would appear. But the good Bavarians didn't
need dancing as an excuse for coitus, as
Joseph Hazzi discovered around 1800 in an
administrative tour of Oberbayern. In the
Seefeld district: "Both sexes are so inclined
to debauchery that you scarcely find a girl
of twenty who's not already a mother."
Around Marquartstein County this interest
in sex nestled within a larger rebelliousness.
The proverb "We'll have no lords" was
popular among people who "get married
enthusiastically and very early, produce lots
of children, among whom sufficient illegitimate ones that this is considered much
more a beneficial than a sinful deed."
Officials in Oberfranken testified in 1833
that communities full of deflowered maidens
were commonplace. "In the countryside a
girl who has preserved her virgin purity to
the age of twenty counts as exceptional, and
is not at all esteemed for it by her contemporaries." In Unterfranken even the "middle
classes" in rural areas, and certainly the
laborers in cities, had by 1839 concluded
"that the natural satisfaction of the sex drive
is neither legally forbidden nor morally very
reprehensible." By 1854 premarital sex had
apparently become so commonplace that
provincial officials were hand-wringing:
"Every time single boys and girls go out
dancing or to some other public enter-
tainment they end up in bed. In places
where male and female servants work side by
side, sexual intercourse is a daily phenomenon; and Altötting County reports that it's

not seen as sinful at all to have produced children before marriage." These are droplets in a torrent. Literate observers were shaken in southern Germany during the first half of the nineteenth century by what they deemed a sexual revolution, first among the youth of the lower classes, and then finally even among those of their own class. . . .

To begin with, what evidence do we have of the infusion of romance into courtship before 1900? For one thing, people either started to say they were in love or to act in ways consistent with no other interpretation. After 1730 there was a big jump in the use of such words as "amour" and "passion" in the explanations that unmarried women gave to municipal officials in Grenoble of why they were pregnant, and there was a decline in the use of such terms as "amitié" that suggests a limited commitment.

In a small town in western France, to take another example, a young journeyman cabinetmaker impregnated the daughter of his employer in 1787, a banal event and in every way "traditional" — save for the young man's remaining in contact with the girl after his flight to avoid prosecution (the traditional seducer would have vanished without a trace), and save for the tenderness of the love letters he wrote. "My dearest, I embrace you with all my heart. I am unable to forget you. Everyday I think of you and hope you do the same for me. Tell me how you feel, if you want to make me happy. I remain your close companion. . . ." Note that the young man was not a peasant but an artisan; for as we shall see, it was outside the agricultural middle class that the revolution begins.

Towards the mid-nineteenth century we learn the following of the coastal town of La Ciotat (Bouches-du-Rhône): "The young men are constantly letting partners with handsome dowries go begging. When they marry, it's ordinarily for inclination and not for advantage. They would be incapable of feigning sentiment they did not feel. Such is the case above all for the young lads who go to sea." So seafaring people, at least, were willing to sacrifice their pocketbooks for their affections. And if it wasn't love, how else may we explain that in a Gascon village, around 1911, "three mailmen became needed instead of two because the posts got so cluttered by all the magazines and postcards the young men and women were in the habit of sending one another"? . . .

The uses of sex. In traditional society, sexuality mainly served instrumental objectives. That is, it helped the participants to achieve ulterior goals of a nonsexual nature rather than serving the exploration of the personality. For traditional unmarried women, especially, intercourse was a means to an end (such as having peace with the employer, or ratifying a marital alliance between two families) rather than an end in itself (sex as personal fulfillment). The testimony we have reviewed suggests that in Europe before 1800, people seldom had sexual intercourse before it was absolutely certain they would marry, and that sex served for them the larger ends of procreation and the continuation of the lineage, rather than being in itself an object of joy and delight. Otherwise the emotionless, passionless, affectionless courtship rituals we have observed would be incomprehensible.

With the first sexual revolution came a breakthrough in intimacy, a dismantling of the sex-role barriers that had hitherto kept men and women locked in watertight compartments with little hope of emotional exchange. The libido unfroze in the blast of the wish to be free. In the years after 1750, lower-class young men and women awakened to the fact that life involved more than just doing your duty in the eyes of the local social authorities and doing your work in the same way that your father had done it, and his father before him. People had personality needs that might conflict with the surrounding community's need for stability. Among these needs was "happiness," and among the cardinal ways of becoming happy was undertaking an emotional relationship with a person of the opposite sex. Such a relationship, of course, meant fooling around, for sex was an obvious extension of emotional intimacy. And so the first sexual revolution would be danced out in the stiff, awkward manner of people who had spent eons in immobility and who were just beginning to create for themselves a sympathetic world of symbols and signs, a culture congenial to romanticism.

The first sexual revolution of the late eighteenth century shifted supervision of courtship from the community as a whole to the peer groups of youth itself. Barriers to promiscuity there had to be — firewalls against the fulmination of all this erotic nitroglycerin that the onrush of sentiment had started agitating — but barriers within the context of a subculture generally sympathetic to self-discovery and intimacy. So there was a lot of sex, and because the youth organizations lacked much of the coercive power of the larger village networks, accidents happened, suitors jumped ship, and illegitimate children were born. Yet the coital partners were doubtless anxious to follow the standards of the larger peer groups of which they were a part.

The second sexual revolution of the 1960s seems to have removed even this feeble peer-group control over adolescent mating and dating. The wish to be free has frayed all the cables that used to tie the couple to surrounding social institutions. Self-realization — accomplished through sexual gratification — has taken command of courtship.

Carl N. Degler

WHAT OUGHT TO BE AND WHAT WAS: WOMEN'S SEXUALITY IN THE 19TH CENTURY

Duncan Crow offers a compellingly witty, articulate portrait; Edward Shorter, an impressive sweep and compelling logic in quite a different direction. Less flamboyantly Carl Degler directly counters Crow by suggesting that important segments of official Victorian culture, in this case American, urged sexual gratification of women as healthy and appropriate. Rather like Branca he attacks convention with a different set of sources, less literary but possibly more widely read and, Degler contends, closer to behavior (and Degler develops more direct evidence in this than did Branca). Degler attacks the same image that Shorter did, but he is really more radical, saying that middle-class women, those presumed pillars of Victorianism, were quiet sexual revolutionaries in their own right, at least by the later nineteenth century. Finally, Degler tries explicitly to deal with the relationship between two sexual cultures and between culture and behavior; for him the combination leaves nineteenth-century women a bit distinctive but far more modern than not.

Despite the apparent agreement between the nineteenth-century medical writers and modern students of the period, it is far from clear that there was in the nineteenth century a consensus on the subject of women's sexuality or that women were in fact inhibited from acknowledging their sexual feelings. In examining these two

Reprinted from Carl N. Degler, "What Ought to Be and What Was: Women's Sexuality in the Nineteenth Century," pp. 1469-1470; 1471-1472; 1483-1484; 1485; 1488. Copyright ©Carl Degler, (from *American Historical Review*, Volume 79, # 5, Dec. 1974). Used by permission.

issues I shall be concerned with an admittedly limited yet significant population, namely, women of the urban middle class in the United States. This was the class to which the popular medical-advice books, of which William Acton's volume was a prime example, were directed. It is principally the women of this class upon whom historians' generalizations about women's lives in the nineteenth century are based. And though these women were not a numerical majority of the sex, they undoubtedly set the tone and provided the models for most women. The sources drawn upon are principally the popular and professional medical literature concerned with women and a hitherto undiscovered survey of married women's sexual attitudes and practices that was begun in the 1890s by Dr. Clelia D. Mosher.

Let me begin with the first question or issue. Was William Acton representative of medical writers when he contended that women were essentially without sexual passion? Rather serious doubts arise as soon as one looks into the medical literature, popular as well as professional, where it was recognized that the sex drive was so strong in woman that to deny it might well compromise her health. Dr. Charles Taylor, writing in 1882, said, "It is not a matter of indifference whether a woman live [*sic*] a single or a married life. . . . I do not for one moment wish to be understood as believing that an unmarried woman cannot exist in perfect health for I know she can. But the point is, that *she must take pains for it.*" For if the generative organs are not used, then "some other demand for the unemployed functions, must be established. Accumulated force must find an outlet, or disturbance first and weakness ultimately results." His recommendation was muscular exercise and education for usefulness. He also described cases of women who had denied their sexuality and even experienced orgasms without knowing it. Some women, he added, ended up, as a result, with impairment of movement or other physical symptoms.

Other writers on medical matters were even more direct in testifying to the presence of sexual feelings in women. "Passion

is absolutely necessary in woman," wrote Orson S. Fowler, the phrenologist, in 1870. "Amativeness is created in the female head as universally as in the male. . . . That female passion exists, is as obvious as that the sun shines," he wrote. Without woman's passion, he contended, a fulfilled love could not occur. . . .

If one can judge the popularity of a guide for women by the number of its editions, then Dr. George Napheys' *The Physical Life of Woman: Advice to the Maiden, Wife, and Mother* (1869) must have been one of the leaders. Within two weeks of publication it went into a second printing, and within two years 60,000 copies were in print. Napheys was a well-known Philadelphia physician. Women, he wrote, quoting an unnamed "distinguished medical writer," are divided into three classes. The first consists of those who have no sexual feelings, and it is the smallest group. The second is larger and is comprised of those who have "strong passion." The third is made up of "the vast majority of women, in whom the sexual appetite is as moderate as all other appetites." He went on to make his point quite clear. "It is a false notion and contrary to nature that this passion in a woman is a derogation to her sex. The science of physiology indicates most clearly its propriety and dignity." He then proceeded to denounce those wives who "plume themselves on their repugnance or their distaste for their conjugal obligations." Napheys also contended that authorities agree that "conception is more assured when the two individuals who co-operate in it participate at the same time in the transports of which it is the fruit." Napheys probably had no sound reason for this point, but the accuracy of his statement is immaterial. What is of moment is that as an adviser to women he was clearly convinced that women possessed sexual feelings, which ought to be cultivated rather than suppressed. Concerning sexual relations during pregnancy he wrote, "There is no reason why passions should not be gratified in moderation and with caution during the whole period of pregnancy." And since his book is directed to women, there is no question that the passion he is talking about here is that of women.

Yet, in the end, there is a certain undeniable inconclusiveness in simply raising up one collection of writers against another, even if their existence does make the issue an open one, rather than the closed one that so many secondary writers have made it. It suggests, at the very least, that there was a sharp difference of medical opinion, rather than a consensus, on the nature of women's sexual feelings and needs. In fact there is some reason to believe, as we shall see, that the so-called Victorian conception of women's sexuality was more that of an ideology seeking to be established than the prevalent view or practice of even middle-class women, especially as there is a substantial amount of nineteenth-century writing about women that assumes the existence of strong sexual feelings in women. One of the historian's recognized difficulties in showing, through quotations from writers who assert a particular outlook, that a social attitude prevailed in the past is that one always wonders how representative and how self-serving the examples or quotations are. This is especially true in this case where medical opinion can be found on both sides of the question. When writers, however, assume the attitude in question to be prevalent while they are intent upon writing about something else, then one is not so dependent upon the tyranny of numbers in quoting from sources. For behind the assumption of prevalence lie many examples, so to speak. Such testimony, moreover, is unintended and therefore not self-serving. This kind of evidence, furthermore, helps us to answer the second question — to what extent were women in the nineteenth century inhibited from expressing their sexual feelinngs? For in assuming that women had sexual feelings, these writers are offering clear, if unintended, testimony to women's sexuality.

Medical writers like Acton may have asserted that women did not possess sexual feelings, but there were many doctors who clearly assumed not only that such feelings existed but that the repression of them caused illness. One medical man, for example, writing in 1877, traced a cause of insanity in women to the onset of sexuality. "Sexual development initiates new and extraordinary physical changes," he pointed out. "The erotic and sexual impulse is awakened." Another, writing ten years later, asserted that some of women's illnesses were due to a denial of sexual satisfaction. "Females feel often that they are not appreciated," wrote Dr. William McLaury in a medical journal, "that they have no one to confide in; then they become morose, angular, and disagreeable as a result of continual disappointment to their social and sexual longings. Even those married may become the victims of sexual starvation when the parties are mentally, magnetically, and physically antagonistic." . . .

[In] the Mosher Survey . . . thirty-five of the forty-five women testified that they felt desire for sexual intercourse independent of their husband's interest, while nine said they never or rarely felt any such desire. What is more striking, however, is the number who testified to orgasmic experience. According to the standard view of women's sexuality in the nineteenth century, women were not expected to feel desire and certainly not to experience an orgasm. Yet it is striking that in constructing the questionnaire Dr. Mosher asked not only whether the respondents experienced an orgasm during intercourse but whether "you *always* have a venereal orgasm?" (my italics). Although that form of the question makes quite clear Mosher's own assumption that female orgasms were to be expected, it unfortunately confuses the meaning of the responses. (Incidentally, only two of the forty-five respondents failed to answer this question.) Five of the women, for instance, responded "no" without further comment. Given the wording of the question, however, that negative could have meant "not always, but almost always" as well as "never" or any response in between these extremes. The ambiguity is further heightened when it is recognized that in answer to another question, three of the five negatives said that they had felt sexual desire, while a fourth said "sometimes but not often," and the fifth said sex was "usually a nuisance." Luckily, however, most of the women who responded to the question concerning orgasm made more precise answers. The great majority of them said that they had experienced orgasms. . . .

In sum, thirty-four of the women experienced orgasm, with the possibility that the figure might be as high as thirty-seven if those who reported "no" but said they had felt sexual desire are categorized as "sometimes." (Interestingly enough, of nine women out of the forty-five who said they had never felt any sexual desire, seven said that they had experienced orgasms.) Moreover, sixteen or almost half of those who experienced orgasms did so either "always" or "usually." As we have seen, in the whole group of forty-five, all but two responded to the question asking if an orgasm was always experienced. Of those forty-three, thirty-four were born before 1875. Five answered "no" to that question without any further comment. One other woman responded "never," and two others said "once or twice." If the "noes" and the "never" are taken together, the proportion of women born after 1875 who experienced at least one orgasm is eighty-two per cent. If the "noes" are taken to mean "sometimes" or "once or twice," as they might well be, given the wording of the question, then the proportion rises to ninety-five per cent. . . .

Much more interesting and valuable than the bare statistics are the comments or rationales furnished by the women, which provide an insight into the sexual attitudes of middle-class women. As one might expect in a population by its own admission poorly informed on sexual physiology, the sexual adjustment of some of these women left something to be desired. Mosher, for example, in one of her few efforts at drawing conclusions from the Survey, pointed out that sexual maladjustment within marriage sometimes began with the first intercourse. "The woman comes to this new experience of life often with no knowledge. The woman while she may give mental consent often shrinks physically." From her studies Mosher had also come to recognize that

women's "slower time reaction" in reaching full sexual excitement was a source of maladjustment between husband and wife that could kill off or reduce sexual feelings in some women. Women, she recognized, because of their slower timing were left without "the normal physical response. This leaves organs of women over congested." At least one of her respondents reported that for years intercourse was distasteful to her because of her "slow reaction," but "orgasm [occurs] if time is taken." On the other hand, the respondent continued, "when no orgasm, [she] took days to recover." Another woman spoke of the absence of an orgasm during intercourse as "bad, even disastrous, nerve-wracking — unbalancing, if such conditions continue for any length of time." Still a third woman, presumably referring to the differences in the sexual rhythms of men and women, said, "Men have not been properly trained." One of the women in the Mosher Survey testified in another way to her recognition of the differences in the sexuality of men and women. "Every wife submits when perhaps she is not in the mood," she wrote, "but I can see no bad effect. It is as if it had not been. But my husband was absolutely considerate. I do not think I could endure a man who forced it." And her response to a question about the effects of an orgasm upon her corroborate her remark: "a general sense of well being, contentment and regard for husband. This is true Doctor," she earnestly wrote. . . .

It seems evident that among these women sexual relations were neither rejected nor engaged in with distaste or reluctance. In fact for them sexual expression was a part of healthy living and frequently a joy. Certainly the prescriptive literature that denigrated sexual feelings or expression among women cannot be read as descriptive of the behavior or attitude of these women. Nevertheless this is not quite the same as saying that the marriage handbooks had no effect at all. To be sure, there is no evidence that the great majority of women in the Mosher Survey felt guilty about indulging in sex because of what they were told in the prescriptive literature. But in two cases that literature seems to have left feelings of guilt. One woman said that sexual relations were "apparently a necessity for the *average* person" and that it was "only [the] superior individual" who could be "independent of sex relations with no evident ill-results." To her, as to St. Paul and some of the marriage-advice books, it was better to indulge than to burn, but it was evidently even better to be free from burning from the beginning. A more blatant sign of guilt over sex came from the testimony of a woman who quite frankly thought the pleasure of sex was a justification for intercourse, but, she added "not necessarily a legitimate one."

V. BIRTH CONTROL

J. A. and Olive Banks

FEMINISM AND FAMILY PLANNING

In a widely cited study of the origins of birth control in Britain, a husband and wife team of sociologists set forth a fairly common view of the early development of this phenomenon. Birth control started in the middle class around 1870. Women were leisured symbols of domesticity; major initiatives were not likely to come from them. Their role and world were in large measure created by men, with whom (in possibly a Victorian version of Shorter's lower-class companionate marriage) they cooperated. Economic pressures on men thus serve as a basic cause, and this vital change in women's behavior arises with no real modification of the conventional Victorian female attitude. Feminism, in particular, had nothing to do with the change. Was the power of Victorian culture, an underlying theme in so many selections in this book, such that basic change could occur only within its premises?

It is easy to see that if the circumstances of the perfect lady were to change in such a way as to threaten the new pattern of life to which she was now accustomed, she might be induced to adopt family planning as a defensive measure. A decline in the supply of domestic servants, for example, might have presented her with the choice between having fewer children or returning to the nursery or kitchen herself. In point of fact, however, she was never faced with such a choice during this period. There was no slackening off in the employment of servants generally, or of nursemaids in particular, until well after birth-control was firmly established. So far as we can tell, there were no changes in the circumstances of the middle classes in the 1870s and after which did not affect husband and wife equally.

There were no special problems facing wives as such.

We may put this differently by asserting that there is no evidence to support the view that emancipation from the traditional pattern of domesticity for middle-class women was carried through in the teeth of opposition from their husbands. On the contrary, all the evidence we have suggests that in the transition to the perfect lady they were assisted and, if anything, encouraged by the men. This indicates that the same may well have been true of the decision to practise some form of family planning, which, far from being a revolt of wives, could have been a joint decision on the part of the married couple acting together. Indeed, in the absence of any evidence that women were successful *at this time* in achieving a greater independence in decision making and in the light of their financial dependence on their husbands, it might well have been the case that the resolve to adopt birth-control was determined by the man alone, and that in this, as in other matters, his wife merely acquiesced. A more plausible approach to the problem, therefore, would seem to be to consider an alternative explanation for the flight from parenthood which might also be regarded as responsible for the changes in the concept of the perfect wife. We can hardly do better at this point than to reintroduce the issue of the relationship between the middle-class standard of living and family size, which has been dealt with in detail elsewhere, and which must now be reconsidered in terms of its bearing on the position of women. . . .

Against . . . [the] background of rising costs of children the middle-class bachelor doubted the wisdom of early marriages. His concern with their cost, of course, must be considered in the light of the general belief that children were inevitable and should be planned for. Granted that babies were, in Matthew Arnold's phrase, 'sent', and might arrive before the marriage had lasted a year, it was perfectly reasonable to postpone the wedding until there were good prospects of supporting not only a wife but a growing family. Accordingly, a young man would be 'accepted on the understanding' that marriage would be delayed until his income was on the upward grade; and for the period after 1850 such an understanding made good sense because, with the economic expansion of the middle classes, he could anticipate a steady series of income increases in the future stretching out before him at least until middle age.

The tendency to postpone marriage, therefore, must be seen as a consequence of the spread of gentility into the middle classes. Although incomes were rising during this period it seems likely that they did not always keep pace with aspirations. Once it was accepted that a young couple should begin their married life at a level which their parents had reached only by middle age, it was impossible to regard early marriage as

anything but imprudent. Moreover, since postponement of marriage was one of the factors responsible for increasing the number of "redundant" women in the population it can be seen that the spread of gentility was itself an indirect cause of the movement to find employment for those middle-class girls and women who had 'no male creatures at hand to keep them'. This aspect of feminism, that is to say, was indirectly a product of the rising standard of living which was so marked a feature of middle-class existence between 1850 and 1870.

Yet, as we have seen, this was in no way a movement to alter the position of the married woman and mother. Indeed, in so far as the spread of gentility was responsible for the development of the idea that the perfect woman should be elegant and leisured, the rising standards resulted not in greater emancipation but in increased dependence upon her husband; and there is no evidence that any but a tiny fraction of wives resented this dependence. It was not yet time for Nora to leave her Doll's House. Women, as much as men, admired the 'womanly woman'. Women, as much as men shrank from the 'strong-minded female'. No doubt there were times when both men and women complained that 'helpless women are such a bore', but they could always comfort themselves with the thought that 'very independent women are not lovable'. There are no signs, even in the 1870's, of the emancipation of women in the home.

It was in the 1870's, however, that the notion of family limitation first began to be widely accepted amongst the members of the upper middle classes. The propaganda of Francis Place in the 1820's had been received with repugnance and his 'To the Married of both Sexes in Genteel Life' had been ignored. Then, after forty years of almost complete silence, a fresh wave of propaganda was started which, culminating in the famous Bradlaugh-Besant trial of 1877 helped to publicise the Neo-Malthusian arguments. Moreover this time, and in spite of the almost hysterical opposition of sections of the press, and the bitter denunciation of the medical profession, there is evidence that sections of the public were now sympathetic to these arguments and ready to implement the notion of positive family planning, even involving recourse to contraception, as opposed to mere postponement of marriage.

Why should the upper-middle classes, so indifferent if not hostile to the idea of family planning before the 1870s, be willing to act upon it afterwards? One possible answer has already been given.

The years of the 1870's and onwards were years of some difficulty for those in receipt of middle- and upper-range incomes. Prices fell, it is true, but incomes suffered something of a set-back too. Servants' wages rose and their labour became more difficult to obtain. Hence, in comparison with the lower middle classes, the better-off sections of society were faced with a greater struggle to maintain and extend the differential standard. The years of what had promised to be inevitable progress had passed away. Some kind of personal planning was necessary now if the social hierarchy was to be preserved.

The rationale is clear. Up to the 1870's the maintenance of gentility, although it frequently presupposed the postponement of marriage, 'did not require the additional notion of the control of births'. Once the young man was fully established in his business or profession, marriage was possible because although children might come at a fairly rapid rate he could always be confident that his income would rise sufficiently to cover his fresh commitments. After 1873 middle-class men and women appear to have thought differently. Their sense of security had been very seriously shaken by the Great Depression and

soon the early optimism of an earlier age died away. For such people postponement of marriage would obviously cease to have appeal for there could be no point in waiting for a prosperity which they were now convinced might never come.

When we look at the flight from parenthood from this point of view it is clear that it was very far from being a revolt of women. Both sexes were concerned to maintain the standard of living to which they had become accustomed, and were ready to accept birth-control to solve their economic problems. Indeed, in so far as the initiative in proposing marriage was customarily a male affair, and in so far as postponement of marriage now gave way to family planning within marriage, it is not unreasonable to argue that the initiative for birth-control came from the men. However, be that as it may, the point remains that neither feminism as such nor the emancipation of the middle-class woman from her traditional role of home-maker were important causal factors in the decline in family size. The case for the overriding significance of the standard of living is accordingly strengthened, especially as this has already been shown to have had important consequences of its own in increasing the need to find incomes for unmarried and widowed women, and hence in strengthening the feminist movement for reform, and at the same time turning the middle-class wife from an economically useful member of the household into an elegant and expensive lady of leisure.

Linda Gordon

WOMAN'S BODY, WOMAN'S RIGHTS

Attacks on the Banks' view were slow in coming; historians seemed convinced that a massive cleavage in sexual and maternal behavior resulted

Reprinted from Linda Gordon, *Woman's Body, Woman's Rights: A Social History of Birth Control in America*, pp. 95-101; 103; 104. Copyright ©1976 by Grossman Publishers, New York.

from prosaic causes perhaps because sex seemed so unimportant to the Victorians as historians saw them. (It could also be noted that smaller families in fact returned to preindustrial tradition, though with contraception rather than high infant mortality rates accounting for relatively few grown children per family.)

Recently Patricia Branca has attacked Banks. Not accepting the myth of the powerless or leisured housewife, Branca sees birth control introduced by women as part of a desire for more control, rationality and pleasure in their lives (see her book, *Silent Sisterhood*). This mentality was not totally unlike that of Shorter's lower-class women — though Shorter himself accepted the Banks view on the origins of birth control.

More recently still another American historian has returned to an effort to associate feminism with birth control at least in the context of the United States, feeling that it would be most compelling if articulate women could be seen at the base of this epochal change (as opposed to Branca's silent, ordinary housewives or the Banks' middle-class husbands). The difficulty in the Gordon approach is a common one in social history: how does one connect often small groups, however articulate, and actual behavior? Divisions among the groups, which Gordon notes, complicate any causal role still further. But there can be little question about what Gordon finds: birth control was a quest by (some) women for female sexual expression and *against* husbands. Interestingly, like the Banks, Gordon accepts the aspects of conventional Victorianism, here not in housewifery so much as sexual morality; many of her pioneers were sexual moderates at best, urging restraint as a birth control weapon. Would many actual Victorian women have gone along with this approach thoroughly enough to produce a significant drop in the birth rate? For Gordon though less completely than for the Banks, behavior basic to the modern woman resulted from Victorian attitudes little changed; actions skirt culture or represent unintended effects of acceptable premises.

By the 1870s the feminist movement in the United States was divided into many different organizations and loose reform tendencies. Yet among these groups there was a remarkably coherent ideology on major questions — marriage and divorce, suffrage, employment opportunity, for example — and on no question so much as on that of birth control. The standard name applied to the demand for birth control was "voluntary motherhood" — incorporating a political statement about the nature of *involuntary* motherhood and child-rearing in women's lives and a solution to the problems they presented.

The feminists who advocated voluntary motherhood were of three general types: suffragists (divided between two national organizations and many local groups), moral reformers (in causes such as temperance, social purity, church auxiliaries, and women's professional and service organizations), and members of small free-love groups. The political distance between some of these feminists was great — as between the socially conservative churchwomen and the usually atheistic and anarchistic free lovers, for example. Thus their relative unity as feminists and voluntary-motherhood advocates seems the more remarkable.

Free-love groups in the 1870s were the closest successors to the perfectionist reform groups of the first half of the century. The free-love movement was always closely related to free thought, or agnosticism, and was characterized by a passionate resentment of the Christian established churches, especially in their power to influence law and create restrictive social and cultural norms. They called themselves free lovers as a means of describing their opposition to legal and clerical marriage which, they believed, stifled love. Free-love groups were always small and sectarian and were usually male-dominated, despite their ideological feminism. They never coalesced into a large or national organization, but represented the dying remnants of a preindustrial period of utopian reform. Their very self-definition built around their iconoclasm and isolation from the masses, the free lovers could offer intellectual leadership in formulating the shocking arguments that birth control in the nineteenth century required.

The suffragists and moral reformers, on the other hand, concerned to win mass support, became increasingly committed to social respectability; as a result they did not generally advance far beyond prevalent standards of propriety in discussing sexual matters publicly. Indeed, as the century progressed the social gap between these people and the free lovers grew, for the second and third generations of suffragists had become increasingly respectable (whereas in the 1860s and 1870s the great feminist theoreticians, such as Elizabeth Cady Stanton, had been intellectually closer to the free lovers, and at least one of these early giants, Victoria Woodhull, was for several years a member of both the suffragist and the free-love camp). But even the quest for respectability did not stifle these feminists completely, and many of them said in private writings — in letters and diaries — what they were unwilling to utter in public.

The similarities between free lovers and suffragists on the question of voluntary motherhood should be understood then not as minimizing the political distance between them, but as showing how their analyses of the social meaning of reproduction for women were converging. The sources of that convergence, the common ground of their feminism, were their similar experiences in the changing conditions of nineteenth-century America. Most were educated Yankees of professional, farm, or commercial families, responding to severe threats to the stability, if not dominance, of their class position. Both groups were disturbed by the consequences of rapid industrialization — the emergence of great capitalists and a clearly defined financial oligarchy, the increased immigration that provided cheap labor and further threatened the dignity and economic security of the Yankees. Above all they feared and resented the loss of their independence and would have undone the wage-labor system entirely had they been able. Free lovers and suffragists, as feminists, welcomed the decline in patriarchal power within families that followed upon industrialization, but they worried, too, about the possible disintegration of the family and the loosening of sexual morality. They saw reproduction in the context of these larger social changes and in the context of a movement for women's emancipation; and they saw that movement as an answer to some of these large social problems. They hoped that giving political power to women would help to reinforce the family, to make the government more just and the economy less monopolistic. In all these wishes there was something traditional as well as something progressive. Their voluntary-motherhood ideas reflected this duality.

Since we bring to our concept of birth control a twentieth-century understanding of it, it is important to stress the fact that neither free lovers nor suffragists approved of contraceptive devices. Ezra Heywood, patriarch and martyr, thought "artificial" methods "unnatural, injurious, or offensive." Tennessee Claflin, feminist, spiritualist, and the sister of Victoria Woodhull, wrote that the "washes, teas, tonics and various sorts of appliances known to the initiated" were a "standing reproach upon, and a permanent indictment against, American women. . . . No woman should ever hold sexual relations with any man from the possible consequences of which she might desire to escape." *Woodhull and Claflin's Weekly* editorialized: "The means they [women] resort to for . . . prevention is sufficient to disgust every natural man. . . ."

On a rhetorical level the main objection to contraception was that it was unnatural, and the arguments reflected a romantic yearning for the "natural," rather pastorally conceived, that was typical of many nineteenth-century reform movements. More basic, however, in the women's arguments against contraception was an underlying fear of the promiscuity that it could permit. And that fear was associated less with any woman's fear for her own virtue than with her fear of other women — "fallen women" — who might undermine her husband's fidelity.

To our twentieth-century sensibility it would seem that a principle of voluntary motherhood that rejects contraception is a principle so theoretical as to be of little real impact. What gave it substance was that it was accompanied by another, potentially explosive, conceptual change: the reacceptance of female sexuality. Both free lovers and suffragists, interestingly, staked their claims here on the traditional grounds of the natural. Free lovers argued, for example, that celibacy was unnatural and dangerous — for men and women alike. . . .

Women's rights advocates, too, began, timidly, to argue the existence of female sexuality. . . . Alice Stockham, a spiritualist and feminist physician, lauded sexual desire in men and women as "the prophecy of attainment." She urged that couples avoid reaching sexual "satiety" with each other in order to keep their sexual desire constantly alive, for she considered desire pleasant and healthful. . . .

The concept of the maternal instinct helped to make Victorian sexual attitudes more consistent. In many nineteenth-century writings we find the idea that the maternal instinct was the female analog to the male sex instinct; as if the two instincts were seated in analogous parts of the brain, or soul. Thus to suggest, as these feminists did, that women might have the capacity for being sexual subjects rather than mere objects, feeling impulses of their own, automatically tended to weaken the theory of

the maternal instinct. In the fearful imagination of the self-appointed protectors of the family and of womanly innocence, the possibility that women might desire sexual contact not for the sake of pregnancy — that they might even desire it at a time when they positively did not want pregnancy — was a wedge in the door to denying that women had any special maternal instinct at all.

Most of the feminists did not want to open that door either. Indeed, it was common for nineteenth-century women's rights advocates to use the presumed special motherly nature and sexual purity of women as an argument for increasing their freedom and status. It is no wonder that many of them chose to speak their subversive speculations about the sexual nature of women privately, or at least softly. Even among the more outspoken free lovers, there was a certain amount of hedging. Lois Waisbrooker and Dora Forster, writing for a free-love journal in the 1890s, argued that although men and women both had an "amative" instinct, it was much stronger in men, and women — only women — also had a reproductive, or "generative," instinct. "I suppose it must be universally conceded that men make the better lovers," Forster wrote. She thought that it might be possible that "the jealousy and tyranny of men have operated to suppress amativeness in women, by constantly sweeping strongly sexual women from the paths of life into infamy and sterility and death," but thought also that the suppression, if it existed, had been permanently inculcated into woman's character.

Modern birth-control ideas rest on a full acceptance, at least quantitatively, of female sexuality. Modern birth control is designed to permit sexual intercourse as often as desired without the risk of pregnancy. Despite the protestations of sex counselors that there are no norms for how often people should engage in intercourse, the popular view always has such norms. Most people in the mid-twentieth century think that "normal" couples indulge several times a week. Given this concept of sexual rhythms, and the accompanying concept of the purpose of birth control, the free lovers' rejection of artificial contraception and "unnatural" sex seems to eliminate the possibility of birth control at all. Nineteenth-century sexual reformers, however, had different sexual norms. They did not seek to make an infinite number of sterile sexual encounters possible. They wanted to make it possible for women to avoid pregnancy if they badly needed to do so for physical or psychological reasons, but they did not believe that it was essential for women to be able to indulge in sexual intercourse under those circumstances.

In short, for birth control they recommended periodic or permanent abstinence, and the tradition of "magnetation" theories of sex among the perfectionists made this seem a reasonable, moderate procedure. The proponents of voluntary motherhood had in mind two distinct contexts for abstinence. One was the mutual decision of a couple. . . . A second context for abstinence was the right of the wife unilaterally to refuse her husband. This idea is at the heart of voluntary motherhood. It was a key substantive demand in the mid-nineteenth century when both law and practice made sexual submission to her husband a woman's duty. A woman's right to refuse is clearly the fundamental condition of birth control — and of her independence and personal integrity. . . .

The insistence on women's right to refuse often took the form of attacks on men for their lusts and their violence in attempting to satisfy them. In their complaints against the unequal marriage laws, chief or at least loudest among them was the charge that they legalized rape. Victoria Woodhull raged, "I will tell the world, so long as I have a tongue and the strength to move it, of all the infernal misery hidden behind this horrible thing called marriage, though the Young Men's Christian Association sentence me to prison a year for every word. I have seen horrors beside which stone walls and iron bars are heaven. . . ." Angela Heywood attacked men incessantly and bitterly; she was somewhat ill-tempered, though not necessarily inaccurate. "Man so lost to himself and woman as to invoke legal *violence* in these sacred nearings, *should have solemn meeting with, and look serious at his own penis until he is able to be lord and master of it, rather than it should longer rule, lord and master, of him and of the victims he deflowers.*" Suffragists spoke more delicately, but not less bitterly. Feminists organized social-purity groups and campaigns, their attacks on prostitution based on a larger critique of the double standard, to which their proposed remedy was that men conform to the standards required of women.

VI. THE LATE NINETEENTH CENTURY: NEW DIRECTIONS?

Lee Holcombe

VICTORIAN LADIES AT WORK

Victoria died in 1901; the nineteenth century ended the year before. But did the Victorian world for women end so quickly? Birth control, and according to some, more radical breaks with tradition in sexual culture and employment, suggest the possibility that women were already striking out in new directions. The following selections, grouped around topics emerging by 1900, suggest more striking innovations. White-collar work commanded increasing attention from employed females; feminism was claiming political equality for women in a number of countries; and the basic grip of Victorian culture on the definition of women's roles can be seen to loosen.

The following selections treat these various developments. All, however, should be assessed against two possibilities. First, that Victorianism, suitably updated and modified, continued to underlie apparently new trends. Disagreements over feminism's relationship to ordinary women include an argument about whether it attacked or in subtle ways expressed Victorian culture. Second, how cohesive was Victorianism in its heyday? Was Victorian culture a monolith that had to be overturned on the way to true modernity? Or was it diverse, perhaps not a culture at all in any complete sense, varying with class and area? Could basic features of women's nineteenth-century development, particularly if already revolutionary against traditional culture, continue in new guise? And, indeed, how new is women's guise even today? How fully has Victorianism been escaped? Here are the basic issues to be assessed against the increasingly public offshoots of women's activities at the end of the nineteenth century.

Lee Holcombe, an American historian, relates the rise of white-collar work in Britain to other new trends such as feminism as well as advanced industrialization. But as "white-blouse" jobs became respectable, was this in new terms or in terms recognizable through the values previously applied to women's employment? It was after all still lower-paid (a more effective cause of women's clerical employment than feminism?) and less prestigious than roughly comparable men's jobs — Holcombe notes that female occupations had a hard time defending strict professional standards. Were these new jobs especially appealing to what women valued in work as well? Here would be new bottles carrying old wine far into the twentieth century. Like birth control, white-collar work might result from a traditional mentality and only later change this mentality in turn.

There were, in fact, frequent alarmed masculine cries that if middle-class women entered the labour market, they would drive men out of work, or at least men's pay would be reduced by the competition of lower-paid female labour. If this were true, some feminists replied, at least it would be fairer to share suffering, to have men take their portion of misery rather than to cast all of it upon women. Others remarked that although women's competition might diminish some men's earnings, women's work would also relieve some men of their financial burdens, for fathers and brothers would no longer have to support their daughters and sisters. But on the whole the feminists believed that the entire community, men as well as women, would gain by women's increased employment. Women must be supported and their maintenance cost the same, whether or not they worked; if they worked, the country would benefit by the increase in its productive power. The amount of work to be done was not a fixed quantity, nor was the "wages fund" of the classical economists; fresh occupations were continually being opened up to educated workers, with the prospect of ever increasing pay. In short, women as well as men could contribute to and benefit from an expanding economy.

The feminists argued their case well, yet leaders are nothing without a following, nor is a philosophy valid without some practical application to the problems of everyday life. The supporters of women's rights might be charged with voicing merely sentimental grievances and with demanding equality for women merely to satisfy their theories, but the charge was never justified, for they were actually addressing themselves to pressing practical problems. Bessie Parkes summed it up: "Except for the material need which exerted a constant pressure upon a large and educated class, the 'woman's movement' could never have become in England a subject of popular comment, and to a certain extent of popular sympathy." The foundations of the Victorian patriarchy did not crumble because of the feminists' verbal assaults, but because the patriarchal ideal departed so far from reality.

A widely read and very influential article which appeared in the *Edinburgh Review* in 1859 was frequently credited with having first shocked the public into an awareness of the problem of "redundant women," that is, the unmarried. It was written by that renowned Radical, Harriet Martineau, whose name for some thirty years had been almost a household word for instructor of the nation in economic and social affairs, and whose words now inspired Jessie Boucherett to found the Society for Promoting the Employment of Women. Drawing upon the census statistics for 1851, Miss Martineau pointed out that there were over half a million more women than men in Britain, single women who could not hope to "marry and be taken care of" and widows who might not have been left provided for by their husbands. Already a sizeable proportion in the mid-nineteenth century, the number of unmarried women increased steadily throughout the period before World War I, the census of 1911 showing that there were nearly 1,400,000 more women than men in the country. (By 1970 women outnumbered men by an estimated 1,500,000. However, whereas females formerly outnumbered males in every age group, they now do not begin to outnumber them till the age of forty-five.) Moreover, this disproportion between the sexes in Victorian times was greater among the middle classes than among the working classes. To illustrate this fact, a woman writer used the 1911 census statistics to compare the number of men and women in six different boroughs of London representing the different social classes: in the three wealthier neighbourhoods (Hampstead, Kensington and Chelsea) there were 5,758 men and 19,738 women, while in the three working-class neighbourhoods (Woolwich, Shoreditch and Bethnal Green) there were 5,185 men and 3,850 women. It was no coincidence that "a period of great upheaval in the female mind" came at a time when there was an "abnormally large" number of unmarried women of "the discussing, thinking, agitating classes."

The chief reason given to explain this surplus of middle-class women was the excessive emigration of men of their class, who were responding to the calls of far-flung empire and seeking new lives in new worlds. As a member of the Army or Navy stationed abroad, a civil servant, a trader, a colonist, the middle-class English male was "anywhere, and everywhere, except where he ought to be, making love to the pretty girls in England." Moreover, contemporaries noted with alarm the growing disinclination of middle-class men to marry, and the tendency among the middle classes to postpone marriage till late in life. Since middle-class women were expected not to work before or after marriage, they were expensive luxuries, contributing nothing to family resources in a period of rising expectations and standards of living. . . .

The wider employment of middle-class women was certainly necessary and even just, but above all it proved to be expedient. England's rapidly expanding economy created a large and increasing demand for labour, a demand which better educated women could supply as well as men — and at a lower cost. (Barbara Bodichon hit upon this last point in an appeal to the self-interest of employers, calling upon them to increase their profits by hiring women workers instead of men, since women expected to receive only about half of men's pay.) The feminists' trust in the country's economic progress and what this would imply for women's opportunities for work was not misplaced, but foreseeing a development is not the same as causing it, and the women's movement cannot be justly credited with bringing about the wider employment of middle-class women. "The great expansion of non-manual [or middle-class] occupations . . . centered on schools, offices, shops and hospitals — an expansion which, deriving from the technological and social diversification of industrialism and satisfying its cheap labour requirements, owed little to pioneering feminists."

Schools, offices, shops and hospitals — these were precisely the places where the early feminists hoped and expected to see an increase in the employment of middle-class women. The growing number of women teachers resulted naturally from the improvements in women's education and, more generally, from the development of a state-supported national system of education. The growth in the ranks of nurses reflected both the progress of medical science and increasing public concern for the health and welfare of the community. The numbers of shop assistants and of clerks swelled to significantly larger proportions of the total working population as a result of the tremendously increased production arising from industrialization and the flourishing state of commerce, nourished by a policy of free trade and the growing wealth and purchasing power of the community. Finally, increasing government activity, itself a response to the growth of an urbanized, industrial society and an awakening social conscience, necessitated the employment of an ever larger army of civil servants. And in three of these fields, shop and clerical work and the civil service, the rate of increase in the number of women employed was substantially above the rate of increase for men, a development which seems best explained, in the final analysis, by the simple fact that women worked more cheaply than men.

Meanwhile, not only were their numbers greatly increasing, but also conditions of work were changing greatly for teachers, nurses, shop assistants, clerks and civil servants. On the one hand, there was a raising of the status of the workers in teaching and nursing, this "professionalization" being a distinctive and widespread phenomenon of the period. The essential feature of a profession has been defined as "special competence, acquired as the result of intellectual training," which "gives rise to certain attitudes and activities." A spirit of solidarity grows naturally among those set apart from the average person by specialized training, and finds formal expression in professional associations. These associations serve as social and educational organizations for their members, and also seek to protect both their members and society at large against untrained practitioners, insisting upon thorough training and recognized tests of proficiency for membership in the profession and enforcing accepted codes of professional ethics. The final step in the evolution or creation of a profession comes with intervention by the government, which sets up a central body, composed of representatives of the profession itself and of the state, to lay down qualifications for admission to the profession and keep a register of those qualified, and to enforce professional discipline by trying those accused of unprofessional conduct and removing from the register the names of those found guilty. Interestingly, it has been suggested that the rise of the professions is one aspect of the democratization or levelling upward of society, a reflection of "the strong desire . . . of the masses . . . to become middle class. . . ."

On the other hand, there was a contrary movement, a sort of "deprofessionalization," among shop assistants, clerks and civil servants, who in the early part of this period had some of the attributes of professionals and unquestionably enjoyed a status of middle-class respectability. A sound general education and an apprenticeship or a probationary training period were necessary for their work. Many of those in the distributive trades and in clerical work could look forward to going into business on their own and thereby achieving an independent position, which is another distinguishing feature of the professional, while civil servants might rise to the highest government posts. But an expanding economy and universal education changed all this. With the growth of large-scale business enterprises, division of labour swept into shops and offices as it had into factories, and shop assistants and clerks tended to be employed increasingly on work of routine nature for which little special

training was necessary, and which offered them little prospect of advancement through promotion and even less prospect of setting up in business for themselves. At the same time, the widening sphere of government activity increased the amount of routine work to be done by civil servants, while regrading of the service tended to confine workers in small compartments with little opportunity of rising to higher posts. Also, with the general improvement in education, men of the middle classes, who had once monopolized these three fields of work, now had to compete for positions both with educated women of their own class and with men and women of the lower classes. In this competitive situation, conditions of work grew worse, and shop assistants, clerks and civil servants tended to sink to the level of a "black-coated proletariat." Their history in the later part of this period is the story of their efforts to improve their lot by means of organization and of government intervention in the form of protective legislation, the two remedies which had done so much to better the position both of the professions and of manual-labour classes.

Inspired, perhaps, by the claims of the women's movement, often hard pressed by material need, and swept onward if not exactly upward by the swelling tide of industrialization, middle-class working women in the later nineteenth and early twentieth centuries drastically altered both their position and their outlook. In the mid-nineteenth century ladies who had to work for their living were a surplus and depressed minority, who were pitied and who pitied themselves. By 1914 middle-class working women, a respected and self-respecting group, were an essential part of the country's labour force.

William L. O'Neill

THE WOMAN MOVEMENT

This comparative study discusses the formation of feminism as a logical, almost calm result of large processes of nineteenth-century modernization. Undergirded by changes in work and family roles, feminism was shaped more precisely by earlier reform movements that provided ideology and political exposure to women (and that conditioned each particular national experience). But might feminism not also be viewed as a reaction to a definite deterioration in the situation of women in the nineteenth century, a deterioration felt particularly keenly within the middle class because of the confinement of Victorian culture? Did feminism, as O'Neill suggests, follow from the dynamic of nineteenth-century changes in the female experience, or was it a passionate statement that the nineteenth century had to be undone?

A ll histories of feminism properly begin with the appearance of Mary Wollstonecraft's *A Vindication of the Rights of Women* in 1792. Scattered attempts had been made earlier in both England and North America to secure a redress of feminine grievances, but with little effect. Miss Wollstonecraft's book was, however, both sensational and ineffective. Although widely read, or, at least, commented upon, it met with universal disapprobation. Coming as it did on the heels of Olympe de Gouges' tract *The Declaration of the Rights of Women* (1789) and Thomas Paine's *The Rights of Man* (1791-92) the book was unpleasantly, and correctly, associated in the English mind with revolutionary France. Even had it not been tainted in this fashion, her *Vindication* would still have fallen on deaf or hostile ears. The English-speaking peoples of her day were quite satisfied with their domestic arrangements, and Miss Wollstonecraft's demands seemed to them unsettling, if not actually immoral. In later years prominent feminists were to call the book their Bible. Inferior as it was to the Scriptures in literary power, it obviously possessed a pertinency and vigour insensible to both modern readers and her own contemporaries. This was her tragedy. Had she been born a generation or two later, when numbers of women were beginning to press against the laws and customs that confined them, her life would have been very different; not necessarily happier, but certainly more productive and more obviously relevant to the needs and interests of her sex. Of course the position of women in 1840 was no worse, and in some respects better, than in 1790, but by this time they were becoming conscious of their disabilities and interested in removing them.

No one can speak with certainty of the reasons why women emerged in the early nineteenth century as a distinct interest group. Few areas of human experience have been more neglected by historians than domestic life, and at this stage we can only speculate about it. In the past it was thought that the family had changed little throughout the Christian era until very recent times. The Victorian family was believed to be, therefore, not a modern institution but the most highly developed expression of an ancient way of ordering domestic life. By the same token such developments as

Reprinted from Willian L. O'Neill, *The Woman Movement; Feminism in the United States and England*, pp. 15-19. Copyright ©1971 by Quadrangle Books, Chicago.

woman suffrage, mass divorce, and the employment of women in large numbers could only be understood as radical departures from the long-established traditions. The trouble with these assumptions is that they do not explain why a family system which had worked so well for so long suddenly came under attack in the nineteenth century. As a rule two explanations have been offered to account for this. In the first place, it is argued, the libertarian sentiments generated by the Enlightenment and the French and American Revolutions gained such force that they came to influence women as well as men. The demand for personal freedom, natural to an egalitarian age, was further stimulated, in the case of women, by an industrial revolution which created jobs for women in great numbers and gave them the opportunities for independence in fact which the rise of liberalism inspired them to demand in principle.

This line of reasoning is plausible enough; it gains strength from the indubitable fact that the first important agitations for women's rights in the 1830s coincided with reform movements in both England and the United States, and came at a time when industrialization was far advanced in one country and well underway in the other. But the problem of timing is more complex than it seems. Why did it take so long for the libertarian sentiments of the Revolution to move American women to action? The first women's rights convention was not held until 1848, nearly three-quarters of a century after the Declaration of Independence was signed. If the prevalence of jobs for women made feminism possible, why were so few leading feminists in both England and America gainfully employed? Middle-class women were least affected by the industrial revolution, but they were the backbone of feminism everywhere. I could go on in this vein indefinitely, but the point is obvious. Simply because certain developments take place at approximately the same time, it does not follow that they are causally related. The ideological argument is in some measure self-justifying, but the influence of the industrial revolution cannot similarly be

taken for granted.

However, there is another way of explaining the origins of feminism that is suggested by Philippe Ariès' remarkable book *Centuries of Childhood*. This historian and demographer argues, mainly on the basis of French materials, that the history of the family is quite different from what we have thought it to be. In his view the medieval family was large, loose, and undemanding. Children were unimportant so long as they were numerous, and all but the poor apprenticed them out at an early age. The family existed chiefly to maintain the continuity of name and property, and its members had relatively few obligations to one another. Men lived in society, not in the family. But, he continues, in the sixteenth century this began to change. Domesticity in the modern sense started to emerge. The family concentrated itself and turned inward, privacy became important, the education of children assumed major proportions, and women acquired a great many new duties and responsibilities. This process, which began with the middle class, was completed in the nineteenth century when all classes developed at least a formal commitment to bourgeois standards of familialism. If Ariès' speculations (and they are rather more than that since he adduces much unconventional evidence to support them) are well-founded, the history of women comes into better focus. Medieval woman enjoyed a considerable freedom. Standards of conduct were broader and more flexible, for noblewomen positions of great authority were not unusual, and even lower-class women enjoyed substantial economic opportunities in certain crafts and trades. By the seventeenth century, however, the old ways were being modified. Although some authorities believe that at least a few women voted as late as the eighteenth century in England, and although they were not specifically excluded from the franchise until 1832, the erosion of their legal and political position seems to have begun with the great jurist Sir Edward Coke (1552-1634). In the seventeenth and eighteenth centuries as domestic life became, from the woman's point of view, more demanding and confining, the alternatives to it diminished. They were squeezed out of certain traditional occupations, and by the early nineteenth-century women, and especially married women, possessed few legal or political rights of their own.

The merit of this hypothesis is that it enables us to see the organization of the family and the status of women on the eve of the Victorian era as the results of processes that were just culminating, rather than as fixed arrangements of great antiquity. So long as the role of women was assumed to have been stable over long periods of time it was hard to explain why in the early nineteenth century it suddenly became onerous. But when we view the position of women in 1800 or 1825 as one that had only recently been established, then the reaction that in fact took place seems perfectly natural, an appropriate if somewhat overdue response to repressive conditions still, in some instances, being formed. The gap between women's narrowed sphere and men's expanding one appears to have reached its greatest extent at a time when liberal and libertarian ideas were in ascendance. In both England and America the exclusion of women became more obvious as the suffrage was broadened, and more difficult to defend. This was particularly true in the United States, as Harriet Martineau pointed out. 'One of the fundamental principles announced in the Declaration of Independence is, that governments derive their just powers from the consent of the governed. How can the political condition of women be reconciled with this?' Even in England, however, where eligibility was more strictly construed, the disenfranchisement of women was becoming less a matter of course. The very Parliament which in 1832 specifically denied votes to women was also the first to debate the issue. Thus, while thinking to put an end to it, Parliament in fact legitimized votes for women as a serious public question. Congress, by way of contrast, was not to recognize woman suffrage as a matter of legislative concern until almost forty years later.

Despite Parliament's initiative in this respect, the emergence of women proceeded more rapidly in the United States – until the twentieth century at any rate. This fact alone casts doubt on the usual thesis that the emancipation of women was a consequence of industrialization. America was much less developed than England in the 1830s, but even at this early date American women enjoyed certain advantages over their English counterparts. It has always been supposed that the frontier circumstances in which many women lived in the early nineteenth century, and which were part of the ancestral experience of most Americans, improved the status of women. Women were scarce on the frontier, and consequently more valuable. In truth, women suffrage prevailed first in the raw Western states, and in Wyoming the territorial legislature specifically hoped thereby to encourage the migration of women. The pioneer woman's legendary courage and fortitude gave the lie to those innumerable assumptions about women's inferior physiology and nervous system that justified their civil disabilities. This did not, of course, prevent most men from continuing to cherish their prejudices and admire their own superior physical and mental constitutions.

Probably of greater importance to American women was the tendency toward association that made such a deep impression upon Tocqueville, and that continues to be so distinctive a feature of American life. In church auxiliaries and missionary societies, and then ir philanthropic and charitable bodies, thousands of women found outlets for their altruism and wider fields of enterprise beyond the domestic circle. Barred from the society of men they discovered among themselves talents and resources enough to advance many good causes and perform many good works. By the 1830s there were literally thousands of separate women's groups holding meetings, collecting funds, discussing public issues, and variously improving themselves. In this manner a revolution of rising expectations was launched. The more women did, the more they wished to do, the more they pressed against the barriers that prevented them from exercising their full powers, and the more eager they became to equip themselves for the tasks ahead. An early expression of this desire was a substantial expansion of educational opportunities. In 1821 the first real secondary school for women was founded in Troy, New York. Later Oberlin College became the first institution of higher learning to admit women and in 1841 produced its first woman graduate. By this time American women were not only better organized than their English sisters, but better educated as well, even though the United States was still comparatively poor and underdeveloped.

Peter Gabriel Filene

HIM/HER/SELF

Focusing on middle class women around 1900, this history of American gender roles outlines the causes and characteristics of what is seen as a major break from the Victorian culture of restraint. This followed from earlier developments such as birth control and better household management; Victorianism shows a clearer hand in criticism of new developments, yet more subtly Victorian traces still distinguished most women from radical youngsters. Evolution more than revolution marked much of the movement into new roles, suggesting the resiliency and variety of nineteenth-century trends. Yet revolutionaries there were, related to new work opportunities, though ironically distracting from political feminism. Ultimately the author finds Victorianism too pervasive and too stultifying; it had to be overturned, and the men who had fostered it had to be attacked. Yet apart from women who were untroubled by continued Victorianism the nineteenth century left its mark in the guilt of those who fled it. Frenzied innovation, muted hostility to men, anguish — is this the ongoing legacy of the nineteenth century?

Women underwent the physical and emotional strain of pregnancy less often, and they typically were in their mid-thirties when the last child went to school. But that was not all of the "extra" life. The average twenty-year-old female of 1900 could expect to live until the age of sixty-four, four years older than her ancestor of a half century before. Thus, mothers could look forward to two decades of life after all the children had left home permanently.

How did women use this new leisure? In decadent self-indulgence, according to some observers. "Too many women are dangerously idle," muttered Edward Bok, the

Reprinted from Peter Gabriel Filene, *Him/Her/Self: Sex Roles in Modern America*, pp. 12-16; 17-19; 20. Harcourt, Brace, Jovanovich, 1974, New York. Copyright ©1974 Peter Filene.

editor of *Ladies' Home Journal*. Without enough to occupy them at home, they were distracting themselves in deplorable ways. There was the matter of fashion, for one thing. The "radical dress reform" at the turn of the century aroused *Harper's Bazaar* to consternation. "What of woman's mission to be lovely?" the editors demanded. "A short-skirted woman on the street, except in a deluge of rain, is a blow to one's ideals. . . ."

But skirts and hats were a trivial debauch compared to the fact that some women were smoking — in public. Etiquette authorities of the 1890s issued clear warning that "the prospects for the future happiness of that young girl are small" who smoked or who even appeared in public with a man who smoked. . . . But prohibition had come too late. Some women were smoking — not only the "advanced" ones, but some of "the most respectable" — at private dinner parties, in restaurants and hotel lobbies, on board ship.

Here was "the new woman," her critics cried, and they denounced her as a traitor to her sex. "Is it to be wondered at," asked Anna Rogers in a widely read article, "that the indefinable charm, the sacredness and mystery of womanhood, are fast passing away from among us?" But the critics were wrong. They cast their indictment too wide. There was a "new woman," but she was not found among the ranks of housewives. Most middle-class mothers did have a new leisure in their middle age, but they were not spending it in Dionysian frolic. Rather, they were discussing Mozart and Chartres and children's playgrounds, at their weekly club meetings, in places as diverse as Watertown, Massachusetts, and Weeping Water, Nebraska. By 1915 the General Federation of Women's Clubs, the national organization that co-ordinated this multitude, could boast a million members or more.

They joined because they found in the clubs a way to escape the loneliness of housework and the emptiness of leisure. But they aspired to more than gossip and bridge. Loyal to the Victorian model of womanhood, they devoted themselves earnestly to "culture." Hence the Shakespeare Club of

Idaho Springs, Idaho, and the Homer Club of Butte, Montana, and the four standard General Federation programs, "The Bible as Literature," "Twelve Famous Novels," "English Poetry of the Nineteenth Century," and "Women in Education." These titles betray the clubs' conservative purposes and practices. Clubwomen were enacting the traditional role that they had hitherto enacted at home by reading sonnets to their children or playing sonatas on the spinet. They were, it seems, merely moving their pedestals to a new location.

They might have come to learn about Hamlet, but they discovered themselves. Although few if any clubwomen intended rebellion against their role, the very experience of organizing as women fostered unintended attitudes. Mrs. Mary E. Rumford, for example, recalled twenty years later "the revelation we clubwomen . . . were to each other" at the first meeting of the General Federation, in 1890. "As one and another appeared upon the platform to give her club report we nudged the neighbor next to us with surprised delight — 'isn't she clever?' 'What wit!' 'How graceful!' 'What sound common sense!' To-day feminine ability does not surprise us. We expect it of clubwomen, but in that earlier day each one gave us a new and peculiar joy."

Heightened self-esteem was the fundamental consequence of membership for most women. While cultivating the aesthetic sensibilities of a lady, they discovered their capacities for organization, public speaking, and intellectual analysis. Most would have been content to stop at this point. But a few carried the implications further, beyond the curtained club windows into the world outside. If the clubs could benefit their own members, they could also benefit others, by applying concerted female energy to the ills of society. So they worked to build public playgrounds, improve street lighting and sewage systems, eradicate child labor, create tuberculosis clinics, expand public libraries, lobby in state legislatures for tenement reforms, and perform a myriad of other activities.

The momentum of club experience took

these leisured middle-class women directly into the male world where, in unladylike fashion, they sought to reform the social injustices neglected or created by men. To this extent they had indeed departed from their traditional role. Yet their reforms stopped short at a significant point — equal suffrage. Not until 1914, after eleven states had granted the vote to women and when passage of the national amendment seemed inevitable, did the General Federation endorse suffrage. This reluctance measures the meaning of the clubwomen's activities. Although most members partly resembled the model of a "new woman," essentially they remained traditional women in a new locale. They did not question the concept of a feminine sphere, only its limits. A few leaders visualized the formation of female political power, but many more preferred political influence. Meanwhile, the rank and file was content with studying art and literature and music.

Ultimately, then, the members had left home, but not woman's sphere; instead, they had stretched the boundaries of that sphere. In the process, they no longer matched the standard portrait of a lady, but remained nevertheless "true women," mothers of the society. Sallie Cotten, president of the North Carolina clubs, neatly defined the limits of female emancipation when she enthused, in a letter to her son, about the type of woman who was "freed from the bondage of an enforced extreme femininity — so-called refined womanhood — and seeing herself as God made her, man's comrade, helper, and stimulator." In short, the clubwomen descended gingerly from their boring idleness on the domestic pedestal in order to fulfill more effectively the role as better half.

Where, then — outside the anxious minds of social critics — was a genuinely "new woman" to be found? Not in the home or the club, but in colleges and professions and "bachelor woman" apartments. Not in the older generation, but in the younger. The new woman was really the new girl or the spinster — a minority of the female minority, but disproportionately conspicuous.

The new girls created the largest commotion. With gusto they went window shopping, attended theater matinées, played tennis or golf, flirted and danced. Household duties, sedentary "culture," chaperones — these girls left them all behind as they romped into the public air with their skirts revealing a full six inches of stockings. They had a bravado that could not be ignored. Indeed, through Charles Dana Gibson's dexterous drawings they became one emblem of the era. "The Gibson girl" was upstaging the lady. . . . Like others of her generation, [the Gibson Girl] is economically self-supporting. "This is a utilitarian age. We cannot sit down to be admired; we must be 'up and doing'; we must leave 'footprints in the sand of time.' "

Silently the lady rises and departs. Behind her, the girl pities this "extinct type." Higher education, she thinks gratefully, has begun to free her sex from the "chains of prejudice." But she has no time for contemplation. "I must be off. I'm due at the golf links at three-fifteen" to meet a man.

This . . . portrays quite accurately the themes dividing the female generations; but in reality the division often was far less verbal, far less polite, far more tumultuous. "Be sure to behave like a lady under all circumstances," Mrs. Mary Thomas wrote to her teenaged daughter, Minnie. "Do nothing that will attract the least notice." Like countless other parents of the later nineteenth century, however, she discovered — gradually and bewilderingly — that something was going wrong. Minnie Thomas insisted on jumping from roof tops too high for even the most daring boy, on dissecting mice, and then on going to college. Maud Nathan's mother discovered her about to crawl along a plank propped between the third-story window sills of two neighboring apartment houses. . . .

Many parents, during the last third of the nineteenth century, were sitting late at night and asking in worried tones: What is the matter with our Mary, our Minnie, our Maud? Why is she so reckless, so rebellious, so intent upon disgrace? They did not find easy answers, nor can we, even with nearly a century of hindsight. A new female generation was coming of age — young women who resisted apprenticeship into ladylike decorum. That much is clear. But why did this new attitude take hold in this era, and why did it inhabit some girls and not others? Here the answers become more various. Explanation begins at the most generalized level, with socioeconomic class. Most of these daughters were growing up in families that had acquired the style of, or at least pretensions to, considerable leisure. Their parents had made a kind of life in which they took quiet pride. They had become substantial citizens, who earned respect for their economic achievements and civic services, and who wanted to pass on to their children the benefits of this status.

But many middle-aged women did not find contentment in their leisure. "I have such nervous attacks without any reason," Mary Helen Smith wrote to her husband from an ocean resort where she and her young daughter were vacationing. "I don't see what should cause them. One day I have a bowel complaint & the next day a headache & I haven't ambition enough even to go to the beach." Here was the sort of malaise so typical, so epidemic, that magazines like *Harper's Bazaar* and the *Ladies' Home Journal* saw the need to publish incessant articles prescribing "self help for nervous women." They advised regular exercise, nutrition, and rest while also imploring the reader to govern her emotions. Meanwhile, Mary Baker Eddy's growing flock of Christian Scientists, imitated by various other spiritual sects, was instructing women with the doctrines of mind cure.

This "nervousness," which modern vocabulary would translate as neurosis, betrayed a profound, unarticulated discontent among many middle-class women. They would not or could not identify it; indeed, denial was precisely why it found mute expression in nerves and bowels and headaches, rather than in vocal protest. They failed to conceal it from their bodies and also from their daughters, who sensed that their mothers had not found a satisfactory

life on the pedestal. Maternal teachings to be a lady carried unconvincing authority when uttered from a sickbed. Without realizing why, the girls ran outside to jump off roof tops or play baseball or watch their fathers at work in the law office, bank, or store.

Even if their mothers were not dis-eased in the role of a leisure-class woman — and certainly many were not — daughters often had difficulty accepting the legacy. In fact, the greater the leisure, the greater the difficulty. After enjoying the privilege of higher education, for example, a young woman easily scorned the whist parties, the afternoon chitchat, the lavish dinners, the clubwomen's "appreciation" of Shakespeare or Liszt. Jane Addams quoted "a happy busy mother" who, while her daughter was performing her daily four hours of piano practice, looked up from her knitting and declared, "If I had had your opportunities when I was young, my dear, I should have been a very happy girl." In response, the girl gazed wistfully at her mother, not daring to speak what was in her heart: "I might believe I had unusual talent if I did not know what good music was; I might enjoy half an hour's practice a day if I were busy and happy the rest of the time. You do not know what life means when all the difficulties are removed! I am simply smothered and sickened with advantages. It is like eating a sweet dessert the first thing in the morning." In this scene Addams was describing herself. She was "filled with shame," she wrote to a friend in 1886; helplessly she was sinking into a "nervous depression. . . ."

As these troubled passages suggest, the girls often were rebelling not in gladness but in anguish, almost despite themselves. Tormented by doubt and shame, they would have welcomed some more conventional role if only there had been one that could have satisfactorily contained their needs. But the conventions of femininity did not fit them. And so they must suffer rebukes — from their consciences and from their elders. The "new girl" became a favorite target of vilification in the public media. Men and women, especially the latter, railed at her hedonism, her conceit, her penchant for discussing risqué topics at the dinner table, her "positively hideous" tanned face and arms, her attempt to "convince the world that she is a man in a different body."

But the vilification was not pure. Mixed in with the abuse was a significantly different tone. Some of these same critics had to admit that they also found delight in this brash daughter of the day. There was something magnetic about a creature who had abandoned the swooning and tears, the fragility, the genteel deference of a lady. Reluctantly the critics confessed "a queer feeling of comradeship." They were saying more about themselves than about the younger generation. They saw the "new girl" enacting the choices that they had been denied or that they had denied themselves. "If I had had your opportunities when I was young, my dear. . . ." It was more than a queer feeling of comradeship; it was a tacit complicity. The "new girls" were rebels-with-consent. Their mothers opposed not with wholehearted disapproval, but with anxious envy; the rebukes served to conceal their guilt about this vicarious transgression of the ladylike role that they had chosen — long ago and irrevocably — for themselves. Via their daughters they were betraying their husbands and, in both senses of the word, betraying themselves.

CONCLUSION

Women have changed in company with the other manifestations of modernization — the growth of cities, factory industry, and white-collar work, and so on. In some cases they seem to have initiated major change on their own account. Granting that the late nineteenth century had not seen the end of this process — some would obviously argue that the twentieth century had to produce a more constructive adaptation, viewing nineteenth century developments as puny, even detrimental — how does woman's modernization seem to shape up?

As the readings suggest, opinions on this can be poles apart. Most women's historians would, to be sure, be tempted to compare the female process to male modernization. Feminists are inclined to stress how male modernization, though perhaps unsuccessful in leaving men dependent on a host of *machismo* devices and lusts for power, shunted women aside. From something like partners women became home bodies, excluded from equal political power or even any political power at all and paid, if working, inferior salaries for inferior jobs. There could be no complete adaptation to industrial and urban change in this situation, for women were truncated beings, compelled to glorify only their functions as wife and mother.

But another school of thought suggests that women met change more constructively than men. Insofar as they were able to preserve and build on certain traditions, such as working mainly at home whether formally employed or not, they were luckier and/or smarter than men, who more thoroughly faced an unfamiliar, cold world outside the family. Within the home as well as in efforts in the broader society, as with the push to win better standards of health, women also innovated. They applied rational methods and new techniques to household chores, to birth control. They won new interests in individual sensual pleasure, notably in greater enjoyment of sex and growing in-terest in their role as consumers. This view, obviously, stresses features of women's nineteenth century that are open to debate. It depends on showing that women were not really fitting the pedestal image, that they had active lives. It assumes a vigorous, constructive womankind, pushing for measures such as birth control, not one repressed by the male world or dependent on men for major initiatives. Proponents of this idea that women did modernize, and modernize with unusual success precisely because they did not or could not follow the male pattern, might stress the increasing gap between female and male longevity opening up during the second half of the nineteenth century. Women had lived on average about a year longer than men in the eighteenth century; by 1900 their advantage from birth was up to four years or more and it was to increase steadily, though male longevity, of course, improved also. Something more than basic biology is involved here. Lack of such great stress; the benefits to female physiology from birth control — whatever the explanation, it seems clear that if one wants to live long, one would do best to be female. Women, furthermore, commit suicide far less commonly than men. Have women, by a constructive balance of radical change and preservation of tradition, learned to cope better than men with the demands of modern life?

Women were repressed and miserable; women were gaining ground steadily — two more different teleologies for nineteenth century history could scarcely be imagined. They clash in their judgment of the satisfactions women could derive from their lives in the nineteenth century itself and in the implications of nineteenth-century trends for the twentieth century. They can be tested in one final area: protest. Women protested less than men did in the nineteenth century, more rarely to be found in riots, revolutions, and particularly in the wave of strikes that swelled at the century's end; probably women shared less equally in protest than in preindustrial European society. One can argue, of course, that this statement misses forms of protest appropriately female such as reform movements, and, of course, one can point to the strong tide of feminism toward the century's end. Some women's historians spend a great deal of time looking for unobvious signs of protest and far more, as the above readings suggest, view the nineteenth century almost as a gigantic staging area for feminism, which at last released the flood of discontent building up during the long previous decades. The view that women did not protest much can, then, be contested. But if they did not, at least until the feminist current grew in force in the countries where it ran strong, what would this mean? Were women, in the main, satisfied, or was their repression so strong and subtle, as in elevation to a vacuous pedestal role, their alienation so individual in nature — the working-class wife venting her anger in slovenly dress and bad housekeeping — that lack of protest is in fact a sign of greater misery? We debate, still, whether to be optimistic or pessimistic about nineteenth-century trends, and the debate applies to any aspect of women's lives that can be captured historically.

There can be no pretense of closing this debate. It is vibrant and significant. It relates obviously to the basic issue of revolution/evolution, in terms of the relation of the nineteenth century to what went before. Assuming that the traditional situation of women was bad, optimists can argue that the revolutions of industrialization and urbanization prompted a female revolution as well, toward the development of a new, healthier, happier woman. Pessimists can admit a revolution, as in work roles, but stress the pain and inequality it caused. Or they may stress evolution: things have never been all that good for women, and the nineteenth century, tying women so closely to tradition while men's standards were changing dramatically, gradually made them worse. (An optimistic evolutionist, a rarer bird at this point, might find traditions such as domestic work sane as well as persistent, giving

women the base for gradual adjustments to change.)

And, of course, the implications for present-day women are immense. The optimist is likely to view the twentieth century as a logical outcome of the nineteenth century: don't worry, sisters, we're on the right track and history is behind us. The sexual revolution in the 1960s was a logical outcome, not because it contradicted but because it built upon earlier trends. Pessimists have a clearer but perhaps grimmer message: we must fight Victorian prudery, inequality, and the like. The focus here is definite but the task arduous, for history must be reversed. We need revolution now. Historical judgments on women's history inform the future, just as history is clearly informed by the present.

But one final word, not to resolve debate but possibly to condition it. Women's history is not total history. It must ultimately be viewed in the light of the history of both genders, of the whole society. Pessimists may easily exaggerate the desirability of trends in male history during the nineteenth century. Were male wage advantages, admittedly present and hotly defended, suitable to compensate for the felt need to yield more and more of the home, of the raising of children, to women? Or when men do indeed seem to gain, does this mean that women somehow lose? Optimists may seize on male trends as well, but with a different selectivity: wage differentials are not so relevant as longevity differentials for example, because women simply did not live to work the way men (misguidedly?) did. Is there not a tendency in both approaches to create a papier-maché man? Man the oppressor, the monopolizer of good things; man the dunce, failing to see that women were quietly creating a more constructive approach to life? Man, in both views, the separate, deciding for his own reasons to put women down or, with the optimists, leaving women increasingly mistresses of their distinctive destinies. Men and women were different in the nineteenth century; role distinctions between the two genders probably increased. But increasing mutuality might develop as well, as in the trend to think, at least, that one was marrying for love. One does not have to view history in competitive gender terms: when man is up, woman is down and vice versa. Ultimately the current debates in women's history are of interest in shedding light on the human, not just the female, condition. Modernization was difficult for people, for men and for women alike. It called for real innovation, it called for appeals to tradition. The balance struck by men and by women may have differed; traditions themselves differed. But the modern man is not totally different from the modern woman either in greater power and happiness or in greater unhappiness. He cannot be, for modern history has intertwined the fates of men and women with fully as much complexity as ever before.

SUGGESTIONS FOR ADDITIONAL READING

General surveys include: Susan Bell, *Women from the Greeks to the French Revolution* (New York, 1973); Elise Boulding, *The Underside of History: A View of Women through Time* (New York, 1976); Patricia Branca, *The X-Factor in History* (London, 1978); and Joan Scott and Louise Tilly, *Women, Work, and Family* (New York, 1978). For national studies: Doris Mary Stenton, *The English Woman in History* (London, 1957); Mary Beard, *Women as a Force in History* (New York, 1971); Elizabeth Janeway, *Between Myth and Morning: Women's Awakening* (New York, 1974); June Sochen, *Movers and Shakers* (New York, 1973); Anne Scott, *The American Woman: Who Was She?* (New York, 1971); Lois Banner, *Women in American History* (New York, 1976); Shiela Rowbotham, *Hidden from History: Rediscovering Women from the Seventeenth Century to the Present* (New York, 1974).

Three essay collections deal with many aspects of women's history: Renate Bridenthal and Claudia Koonz, *Becoming Visible: Women in European History* (New York, 1976); Mary Hartman and Lois Banner, eds., *Clio's Consciousness Raised: New Perspectives on the History of Women* (New York, 1974); Martha Vicinus, ed., *Suffer and Be Still: Women in the Victorian Age* (Bloomington, Indiana, 1972).

On women's work: Patricia Branca, "A New Perspective on Women's Work; A Comparative Typology," *Journal of Social History* 17.#1 (Winter 1975), pp. 129-153; Theresa McBride, *The Domestic Revolution: The Modernization of Household Service in England and France*, 1820-1920 (New York, 1976); Margaret Hewitt, *Wives and Mothers in Victorian Industry* (London, 1958); Ivy Pinchbeck, *Women Workers in the Industrial Revolution* (London, 1931); Betty Sheild, *Women in Norway; Their Position in Family Life, Employment and Society* (London, 1970). An important general statement, examining trends in the Third World, is Ester Boserup, *Woman's Role in Economic Development* (New York, 1970).

On family life and sex: John Haller, *The Physician and Sexuality in Victorian America* (Urbana, 1974); Stephen Marcus, *The Other Victorians* (New York, 1965); Norman E. Himes, *Medical History of Contraception* (Baltimore, 1936); J. A. Banks, *Prosperity and Parenthood* (Liverpool, 1954); Shirley Green, *The Curious History of Contraception* (London, 1971); Patricia Branca, *Silent Sisterhood* (Pittsburgh, 1975).

Materials from which selections were taken are not cited here, though further reading in them would benefit any additional study in women's history.

F-H

STEARNS, F

The Rise o

Forum Pres

65 pages